Everyday
Assessment

in the Science Classroom

SCIENCE EDUCATORS' ESSAY COLLECTION

Everyday Assessment

in the Science Classroom

Edited by J Myron Atkin and Janet E. Coffey

NATIONAL SCIENCE TEACHERS ASSOCIATION
Arlington, Virginia

Claire Reinburg, Director
J. Andrew Cocke, Associate Editor
Judy Cusick, Associate Editor
Betty Smith, Associate Editor

ART AND DESIGN Linda Olliver, Director
NSTA WEB Tim Weber, Webmaster
PERIODICALS PUBLISHING Shelley Carey, Director
PRINTING AND PRODUCTION Catherine Lorrain-Hale, Director
    Nguyet Tran, Assistant Production Manager
    Jack Parker, Desktop Publishing Specialist
PUBLICATIONS OPERATIONS Erin Miller, Manager
sciLINKS Tyson Brown, Manager
    David Anderson, Web and Development Coordinator

NATIONAL SCIENCE TEACHERS ASSOCIATION
Gerald F. Wheeler, Executive Director
David Beacom, Publisher

Science Educators' Essay Collection
Everyday Assessment in the Science Classroom
NSTA Stock Number: PB172X

05 04 03 4 3 2 1

Library of Congress Cataloging-in-Publication Data
Everyday assessment in the science classroom / J. Myron Atkin and Janet E. Coffey, editors.
    p. cm.— (Science educators' essay collection)
Includes bibliographical references and index.
ISBN 0-87355-217-2
1. Science—Study and teaching (Elementary) —Evaluation. 2. Science—Study and teaching (Secondary)—Evaluation. 3. Science—Ability testing. I. Atkin, J. Myron. II. Coffey, Janet E. III. National Science Teachers Association. IV. Series.
LB1585.E97 2003
507'.1—dc21   2003000907

Contents

1 **The Importance of Everyday Assessment**

Paul Black 1

Assessment for learning is set in the context of conflicts and synergies with the other purposes of assessments. The core ideas are that it is characterized by the day-to-day use of evidence to guide students' learning and that everyday practice must be grounded in theories of how people learn. Its development can change the classroom roles of both teachers and students. The ways in which practice varies when broad aims of science education change are illustrated in relation to practices in other school subjects.

2 **Learning through Assessment: Assessment *for* Learning in the Science Classroom**

Anne Davies 13

This chapter presents an extended example from a middle school science classroom of what assessment that supports learning looks like. In the example, the teacher models assessment for learning by talking about learning with her students; showing samples of quality work; setting and using criteria; helping students self-assess and set goals; providing specific, descriptive feedback; and helping students to collect evidence of learning and to use that evidence to communicate with peers and adults.

3 **Examining Students' Work**

Cary I. Sneider 27

Examining student work is an essential aspect of teaching, yet it is easy to miss opportunities to learn about how students are interpreting—or misinterpreting— the lessons we present to them. In this chapter the author shares insights concerning the techniques he has found to be most effective in tuning in to his students, so that he can adjust his teaching methods and content in order to be a more effective teacher.

This chapter provides an overview of frameworks that teachers can use to conduct assessments of students' engagement in scientific inquiry. The author examines two factors that are central to such assessment. One factor is the design of classroom learning environments, including curriculum and instruction. The second factor is the use of strategies for engaging students in thinking about the structure and communication of scientific information and knowledge. The chapter includes an up-to-date description of nine National Science Foundation–supported inquiry science units.

Questioning can be used to probe for understanding, to initiate inquiry, and to promote development of understanding. The results from questioning, listening, and assessment also can be used by teachers to promote their own growth as professionals. This chapter presents a transcript of a class discussion in which questioning is used to assess and foster student thinking. After developing this context for questioning, the authors discuss purposes and kinds of questions, then revisit the context to demonstrate how the results of assessment through questioning can be used to guide the adaptation of curriculum and instruction.

While much of the responsibility for classroom assessment lies with teachers, students also play an important role in meaningful assessment activity. Bringing students into the assessment process is a critical dimension of facilitating student learning and in helping to provide students with the tools to take responsibility for their own learning. The author examines the role students can play in assessment through a closer look at a middle school program where students actively and explicitly engage in all stages of the assessment process.

As science education moves increasingly in the direction of teaching to standards, teachers call for classroom assessment techniques that provide a richer source of "rigorous and wise diagnostic information." Student-to-student comparisons and single grades are no longer enough, and here the authors describe a new type of criterion-based assessment to track individual learning trajectories. It can be embedded in the curriculum, easily used in the classroom, customized by grade level, subject area, and standard set, and controlled by the classroom teacher.

Professional development related to everyday classroom interactions can require a shift in the teacher's priorities in the classroom from a focus on managing activity and behavior to a mind-set of managing learning opportunities. This essay looks closely at a professional development approach that sees the teacher not only as a professional engaged in learning and implementing new strategies for assessing students, but also as an individual who is undergoing personal change in beliefs.

In contrast to classroom assessments that can provide immediate feedback in the context of ongoing instruction, large-scale assessments are necessarily broader survey instruments, administered once-per-year and standardized to ensure comparability across contexts. Classroom and large-scale assessments must each be tailored in design to serve their respective purposes, but they can be symbiotic if they share a common model of what it means to do good work in a discipline and how that expertise develops over time. Three purposes of large-scale assessment programs are addressed—exemplification of learning goals, program "diagnosis," and certification or "screening" of individual student achievement. Particular attention is given to the ways that assessments should be redesigned to heighten their contribution to student learning. In addition, large-scale assessments are considered as both the site and impetus for professional development.

As a context for thinking about the claims made in this book, some of the circumstances that have influenced the demand for and character of assessment in general are noted. The argument is then made that the substantial lack of coherence in today's assessment scene is due in large part to policies and practices that fail to recognize that there is no one best approach to assessment and that assessment and purpose must be closely coupled.

Acknowledgments

We wish to acknowledge our debt to Rodger Bybee and Harold Pratt. A National Science Teachers Association (NSTA) "yearbook" was Rodger's vision, and he served as the editor of the first volume, *Learning Science and the Science of Learning*. Rodger and Harold helped to identify classroom assessment as a focus for a subsequent volume. Their discussions were the impetus for this collection. Many people within the NSTA organization supported the launch of the annual series and this volume—particularly Gerry Wheeler, executive director of NSTA, and David Beacom, NSTA publisher. We also thank Carolyn Randolph, current NSTA president, for her support.

The authors of the separate chapters have been extraordinarily responsive to suggestions from us and from the reviewers and have made their revisions in a timely manner. Their dedication to improving science education and their desire to engage in a dialogue with and for teachers are inspiring.

We also thank the following individuals for their reviews of this volume:

Ann Fieldhouse, Edmund Burke School, Washington, D.C.
Patricia Rourke, Potomac School, McLean, Virginia
Rick Stiggins, Assessment Training Institute, Portland, Oregon

The reviewers provided thorough and thoughtful feedback. The volume is better for their efforts.

Special acknowledgments are due for Claire Reinburg and Judy Cusick at NSTA. Claire initiated early communication and helped with logistics from the outset. Judy Cusick has provided support in innumerable ways, not least as careful production coordinator for the entire volume. Claire and Judy have guided us smoothly through the process, coordinated reviews, and served as invaluable resources. We thank them both for their time and effort.

Although the reviewers provided constructive feedback and made many suggestions, they did not see the final draft before release. Responsibility for the final text rests entirely with the chapter authors and the editors.

About the Editors

J Myron (Mike) Atkin is a professor of education and human biology at Stanford University. He directs the National Science Foundation–supported Classroom Assessment Project to Improve Teaching and Learning (CAPITAL) at Stanford. He formerly chaired the National Research Council committee that prepared an addendum to the National Science Education Standards on assessment in the science classroom. In addition to having taught at the elementary and secondary school levels, he has served as dean of education at both the University of Illinois and at Stanford. For much of his career, he has emphasized the central role of teachers in designing high-quality science education programs and now focuses on strengthening that role in any comprehensive system of assessment and accountability.

Janet E. Coffey, a former middle school science teacher, currently works with teachers on the Classroom Assessment Project to Improve Teaching and Learning (CAPITAL) at Stanford University. CAPITAL is a National Science Foundation–funded effort that seeks to better understand teachers' assessment practices as they strive to improve their practices. She worked at the National Research Council as a staff member on the development of the National Science Education Standards. She earned her Ph.D. in science education from Stanford University.

Introduction

J Myron Atkin and Janet E. Coffey

The assessment that occurs each day in the science classroom is often overlooked amidst calls for accountability in education and renewed debates about external testing. We believe that daily assessment should be moved to the foreground in these broad discussions and receive greater attention in policy circles. Research points to the positive influence that improved, ongoing classroom assessment can have on learning. Documents that offer visions for science education—such as the *National Science Education Standards* (NRC 1996) and materials associated with Project 2061 (AAAS 1993)—strongly echo that sentiment.

Too often, assessment is used synonymously with measurement (in the form, for example, of tests and quizzes). The misconception that they are the same minimizes the complexity and range of purposes of assessment. As teachers are aware, assessment in any classroom is rich and complicated. It includes tests and quizzes, of course, but also students' other work, students' utterances made while conducting lab investigations, and class discussions in which students share their explanations for what they have observed. It raises issues of quality and of what counts as evidence for learning. It happens in reflection, in exchanges that occur countless times a day among teachers and students, and in feedback on work and performance. When we reduce assessment to a specific event or "thing"—the test, the lab practical, the grade—it is easy to overlook the interactive assessment that occurs each day in the classroom.

Assessment operates to improve student learning, not solely measure it, when it is used to move the student from his or her current understanding to where the student would like to be (or where the teacher would like the student to be). To cross that gap, the teacher and student must *use* feedback from assessments. Quality and use of information become crucial in that process. Sometimes the way to bridge that gap is clear, with obvious starting and destination points. Sometimes, however, it is rendered more complex when the destination point is not so clear, as in inquiry-based science investigations. In inquiry learning, students ask their own questions and face multiple paths to answering those questions. Students must continually reflect on what they are doing and ask themselves, Where am I now? Where do I need to go? How do I get there? What is my evidence?

Everyday assessment is local and contextual. It depends more on the skills, knowledge, attentiveness, and priorities of teachers and students than on any particular set of protocols or strategies. Opportunities for meaningful assessment occur numerous times each day—within interactions, in conversations, by way of observations, and even as part of traditional assessment. A test review or a discussion about criteria of good lab reports each provides opportunities for assessment-related conversations. When the K–12 teacher attends closely to questions and responses and observes students as they engage in inquiry, he or she will gather important assessment information on a daily basis.

The challenge for teachers and students is to maintain a classroom assessment culture that supports learning for *all* students. In this culture, teaching and assessment are so closely entwined that the two become difficult to differentiate; students engage actively and productively in assessment; clear, meaningful criteria exist; and teachers provide high-quality, regular feedback. In classrooms with supportive assessment cultures, the focus is on learning rather than on grades, on progress rather than on fixed achievement, on next steps rather than on past accomplishments. Achievement and accomplishments serve an assessment purpose, as can grades; however, they alone do not assessment make.

In any discussion of assessment, issues associated with teaching, learning, and curriculum quickly arise, as do questions of equity, fairness, and what counts as knowing and understanding. These interconnections, after all, constitute one reason that the topic of assessment is so important. In this volume, the authors address the interconnections and provide guidance and illuminate challenges—at the same time that they maintain a sense of the bigger picture. Although our primary audience is classroom teachers, we also hope that this book will be informative and useful to those who work with teachers, in either professional development or teacher education capacities, and to school administrators, program designers, policy makers, and parents.

In Chapter 1, Paul Black frames the assessment that occurs every day in the classroom within the broader realm of assessment and its multiplicity of purposes. For everyday assessment to contribute to improved learning, he argues, action must be taken based on evidence. This action could come in any number of forms, not the least of which include altering teaching, modifying curriculum, or providing students with useful feedback. Even the most informative data do little good to students and teachers if the data do not feed into learning activities. Black provides an overview of some theoretical assumptions embedded in a view of assessment that supports learning, and he highlights issues related to assessment in science classrooms. He also addresses the tensions and synergistic opportunities that exist when trying to manage the many purposes assessment must serve.

In Chapter 2, Anne Davies discusses the critical role teachers play in ongoing assessment. Teachers not only identify and articulate learning goals, they also find samples of work to meet those goals, consider the type of work that would serve as evidence of attainment, and assist students in developing an understanding of the goals. Her discussion highlights the relationships among assessment, curriculum, and teaching. As we see in many of these chapters, the three topics are, at times, difficult to distinguish from one another.

Cary Sneider, author of Chapter 3, examines what can be gained through careful consideration of student work, which includes what students do, say, and produce. Through reflecting on his own career as a teacher, which began as an Upward Bound tutor, his work as a curriculum developer, and now his present position in an education department at a science museum, Sneider makes a case for tuning into what students do and say to gain insights into the nature of their ideas and understandings. He reminds us that to teach is not necessarily to learn. Assessment serves as a critical link between the two processes. In this essay, Sneider encourages teachers to move beyond the use of written responses and final products and to see the value of listening to, conversing with, and observing students as they engage in activities as well.

The focus of Chapter 4 is on assessing inquiry science. Richard Duschl offers a metaphor of "listening to inquiry" to guide teachers as they support inquiry in their classrooms. The organic nature of inquiry excludes more traditional tests as a means of helping students move forward in pursuit of investigation. With inquiry, there are few clear destinations or explicit goals toward which to steer. Duschl looks at the design of learning environments that engage students in thinking about the structure and communication of scientific ways of thinking. Deliberations about what counts as data, evidence, and explanation would give inquiry a voice, to which student and teacher alike can listen.

Chapter 5 explores issues related to questioning in the classroom. Specifically, Jim Minstrell and Emily van Zee highlight the importance of developing and asking questions that help students consider scientific phenomena and elicit thoughtful and in-depth responses that reveal insight into student understandings. The authors discuss ways in which these insights can be used by teachers to plan additional activities, modify existing ones, and inform future questions. A message that emerges in this chapter is the important role that subject matter plays when teachers are listening to student responses and following those responses with further questions.

Much of the classroom assessment literature focuses on the roles of teachers. Chapter 6 shifts the focus to students. Janet Coffey addresses the integral role students can play in everyday classroom assessment. Student participation in and with assessment activities can help clarify and establish standards for quality work and help students to identify the bigger picture of what they are learning. Through lessons learned from a middle school program where students had opportunities and expectations to participate actively in assessment, Coffey identifies ways to support students as they become self-directed with respect to assessment.

Mark Wilson and Kathleen Scalise take on issues related to grading in Chapter 7. Grades quickly can become the centerpiece of any discussion of assessment at the classroom level. Wilson and Scalise discuss the meanings that underlie grades, the information they convey, and what they often represent. Grades, they argue, often reflect a teacher's perception of a student's effort rather than what the student has learned. Any time a large amount of information is reduced to a single letter grade, much of the useful information behind the grade gets lost. The authors offer a framework for assessment tools that can generate useful assessment data for classroom purposes and for reporting purposes. Assessment tools such as the ones they share can yield useful and high-quality assessment data for teachers, students, parents, and other interested parties. An element of their model includes teacher "moderation meetings," where teachers discuss student work, scores, and interpretations. These deliberations can provide powerful professional development opportunities.

In Chapter 8, Mistilina Sato discusses assessment-related professional development for teachers. She advocates for a change in the teacher's image from that of monitor and maker of judgments to that of manager of learning opportunities. For lasting change, she argues, teacher professional development must go beyond learning new strategies and skills to take into consideration the teacher as a person. Sato points out that teachers enter the classroom as individuals with beliefs, values, backgrounds, assumptions, and past experiences that shape who they are in the classroom and the actions they take. Reform efforts that overlook these personal dimensions of teachers will find minimal success. She shares lessons from a National Science Foundation–funded assessment effort currently underway with Bay Area middle school science teachers.

Lorrie Shepard explores the assessment landscape beyond the classroom in Chapter 9. Specifically, she discusses the ways in which large-scale assessment could be redesigned to heighten contributions to student learning. Even within the realm of large-scale, external testing, a myriad of purposes clamor for attention. Due to constraints such as time and cost, these assessments often take the form of traditional tests. Shepard points out that all tests are not the same. The intended purposes of a test shape the content, criteria for evaluating, and technical requirements; all needs cannot be met through a single test. Shepard calls for external tests to embody important learning goals, such as those set forth in the National Research Council's *National Science Education Standards* (1996) or AAAS's *Benchmarks for Science Literacy* (1993). Examples of actual efforts underway in districts and states help show possibilities for lessening tensions.

James Rutherford provides a historical overview of educational assessment and reform in science education in Chapter 10. The shifting focus of school, district, and national reform efforts has made sustained attention to any one initiative difficult and frustrating at best. Assessment is no exception. We are quick to react to "crises"—real or imagined—rather than take proactive steps, with a long-term view and guidance from solid research literature, toward higher quality science instruction. Rutherford proposes that teachers, parents, and others within the educational community assess assessments by asking critical questions about the assessments as well as the information they provide. He concludes his chapter by offering questions for all of us to consider. In doing so, he sets a frame for use of this book as a tool for professional development. Generating discussion among teachers about some of the ideas raised and addressed in any or all of these chapters would be a valuable outcome of the book.

As Rutherford indicates, this collection may raise more questions than it answers. We, too, hope that this volume contributes to the practical and professional development needs of teachers. We hope it illuminates the importance of attending to everyday assessment, raises issues worthy of reflection and consideration, and offers some practical suggestions. Thinking and acting more deliberately with regard to the ongoing assessment that occurs each and every day in the classroom can go a long way to making our classrooms more conducive to learning for all students.

References

American Association for the Advancement of Science (AAAS). 1993. *Benchmarks for science literacy*. New York: Oxford University Press.

National Research Council (NRC). 1996. *National science education standards*. Washington, D.C.: National Academy Press.

The Importance of Everyday Assessment

Paul Black

Paul Black is Emeritus Professor of Science Education at King's College London. He retired in 1995, having spent much of his career in curriculum development and research in science education. In 1987–1988 he was chair of the government's Task Group on Assessment and Testing, which set out the basis for the United Kingdom's national testing. More recently, he has served on advisory groups of the National Science Foundation and is a visiting professor at Stanford University. His recent research with colleagues at King's has focused on teachers' classroom assessments. This work has had a significant impact on school and national policies in the UK.

The Context: Conflicts and Synergies of Purpose

If assessment is understood in a broad sense—that is, to signify all those processes and products that provide evidence about what is happening—it is immediately evident that in education, assessments are all-pervasive. They influence, even rule, the context within which teachers work, but are also an essential part of the everyday minutiae of teachers' work with their students. This broad interpretation leads to a need to impose some structure on any discussion, so I start here with a discussion of purposes of assessment.

Three main purposes can be distinguished. Assessment can serve *accountability*, *certification*, or *learning*.

- For *accountability*, the evidence has to be broad in scope and designed to highlight needs that might be met through policy actions. This purpose can be served by testing samples of the student population, as well as by collecting a range of other data so that interpretation might be served by exploring interrelationships. Such a broad program might be called an evaluation, to distinguish it from assessment, which is seen as only one of its components. Such surveys as the National Assessment of Educational Progress (NAEP), the Third International Mathematics and Science Study (TIMSS), and the Program for International Student Assessment (PISA) are examples. However, an *accountability* exercise can be designed for a different purpose—to drive improvement by linking the results to public exposure and other rewards or punishments. It is usual, albeit unnecessary, to test every student.

- For *certification*, the audience is the individual students and those who care about them, together with potential employers and those controlling admission to the further stages of education. For both *accountability* and *certification,* the evidence is often limited to results of formal written tests drawn up and marked by agencies external to the school. However, it is possible, and indeed normal in some countries, to use evidence provided from within schools to help meet these purposes. The collection of evidence need not then be limited to formal, timed tests; the broader term assessment is then appropriate.

- For *learning,* the dominant term can be assessment, but evaluation and diagnosis sometimes creep in. The purpose is clear enough in principle, while action based on the evidence can range from minute-by-minute feedback to adjustment of the lesson plans for next year.

Over all of this spectrum, the concepts of *reliability* and *validity* are central. To claim reliability, one has to be sure that if the student were to take a parallel form of the same assessment on another occasion, the result would be the same. This claim is rarely supported by comprehensive evidence. For certification, and internal school decisions about tracking and grading, weak reliability is serious because the effects on students are hard to reverse. In assessment for learning, reliability is harder to achieve, but it is less serious an issue provided that the teacher's approach is flexible so that the effects of wrong decisions can be discerned and corrected within a short time.

Validity is a more serious issue. The key to the concept is that the inferences that are made on the basis of an assessment result are defensible (Messick 1989). In the case of a formal written test, any inference that goes beyond saying that the student did well on this test on this date requires justification. But inferences do go far beyond such limitation, for it is often assumed that the student could do well in any test in any part of the subject on any occasion in the future, understands the nature and structure of the subject, is competent in exercising the discipline of the subject, and is well-equipped to benefit from more advanced study.

One source of the limitation on validity is that formal tests have to be short and inexpensive to administer and mark. However, many aspects of understanding and competence can only be displayed over extended periods of time in unconstrained conditions. It is often claimed that a written test might serve as a surrogate for such activity, but those claims usually lack empirical support (Black 1990; Baxter and Shavelson 1994). For this reason, significant efforts have been invested in developing a broader range of methods of assessment—for example, new types of evidence for performance (e.g., notebooks written by students about a science investigation) and new procedures to improve and attest to the evidence that teachers can gather from their more extensive interactions with their students. However, what then needs to be made clear is whether these innovations are designed to serve *accountability* and *certification,* or to serve *learning,* or to serve all three purposes.

Demands of accountability are often seen to impose such high-stakes pressures on teachers that assessment for learning is not seriously considered. When the public believes that wholly external written tests are the only trustworthy evidence for students' achievement, and then teachers believe that the pressures to succeed can only be met by ad hoc and inadequate methods of learning, dominance of the accountability purpose seems inevitable. Yet critical scrutiny of the claims for the superiority of formal tests is not supported by careful scrutiny of their reliability and validity. It has been demonstrated that when any such test is newly introduced, performances will rise steadily for a few years and then level out. If the test is then changed, performance will drop sharply and then rise again to level off in a further few years (Linn 2000). Thus, the high-stakes performances that ensue are, at least in part, artifacts of the pressures of the particular test being used rather than valid educational measures. Ironically, the belief of most teachers that they have to "teach to the test" rather than teach for sound understanding is also unjustified, for there is evidence that the latter strategy actually leads to better performances even on the tests to which the former, narrow teaching approach is directly aligned.

The problem for policy makers is to stand back from current assumptions and radically rethink their approach to reconciling the different purposes of assessment. A key feature of any such appraisal must be to strengthen teachers' own skills in assessment so that the public can have confidence in the capacity of teachers to serve all three purposes in a valid and rigorous way. The problem for teachers and schools is to improve practices, to be clear about the purposes that those practices are designed to serve, and to resolve any conflicts as best they can within today's constraints.

How Do People Learn?

Three common assumptions about learning, which have their origins in behaviorist psychology (Collins 2002), are that (1) a complex skill can be taught by breaking it up and teaching and testing the pieces separately; (2) an idea that is common to action in many contexts can be taught most economically by presenting it in abstract isolation so that it can then be deployed in many situations; and (3) it is best to just learn about new things first and not try for understanding—that will come later. A test composed of many short, "atomized," out-of-context questions and the practice of "teaching to the test" are both consistent with those assumptions.

Contemporary understanding of the ways that children learn looks at the process quite differently (Wood 1998). A first important lesson is illustrated by the following quotation:

> ... even comprehension of simple texts requires a process of inferring and thinking about what the text means. Children who are drilled in number facts, algorithms, decoding skills or vocabulary lists without developing a basic conceptual model or seeing the meaning of what they are doing have a very difficult time retaining information (because all the bits are disconnected) and are unable to apply what they have memorized (because it makes no sense). (Shepard 1992, 303)

Current "constructivist" theories focus attention on the models that a learner employs when responding to new information or to new problems. Even for the restricted task of trying to memorize something, one can do better if one already has some scheme built on relevant understanding and tries to link the new knowledge with existing patterns. It appears that memory is rather like a filing cabinet—that is, the storage is only useful insofar as the filing system makes sense so that one knows where to look.

More generally, learning always involves analyzing and transforming any new information. Piaget stressed that such transformation depends on the mind's capacity to learn from experience—within any one context, we learn by actions, by self-directed problem-solving aimed at trying to control the world. Abstract thought evolves from such concrete action. It follows that

> *... teaching that teaches children only how to manipulate abstract procedures (e.g., learning how to solve equations) without first establishing the deep connections between such procedures and the activities involved in the solution of practical concrete problems (which the procedures serve to represent at a more abstract level) is bound to fail.* (Wood 1998, 9)

Here, context is important. An individual's general capacity for abstract thought may be exhibited in, say, family relationships but be quite absent in, say, physics concepts. It is also evident that transformations of incoming ideas can only be achieved in light of what the learner already knows and understands, so the reception of new knowledge depends on existing knowledge and understanding. It follows that

> *... learning is enhanced when teachers pay attention to the knowledge and beliefs that learners bring to a learning task, use this knowledge as a starting point for instruction, and monitor students' changing conceptions as instruction proceeds.* (Bransford, Brown, and Cocking 1999, 11)

Research in the learning of science has shown that many learners resist changes in their everyday and naive views of how the natural world works, despite being able to play back the "correct" science explanations in formal tests. So teaching must start by exploring existing ideas and encouraging expression and defense of them in argument, for unless learners make their thinking explicit to others, and so to themselves, they cannot become aware of the need for conceptual modification. The next step is to find ways to challenge ideas, usually through examples and experiences that are new to pupils and that expose the limitations of their ideas. It follows that assessment for learning must be directed at the outset to reveal important aspects of understanding and then be developed, within contexts that challenge pupils' ideas, to explore responses to those challenges.

Such classroom activities can be a basis for learning development at a more strategic level. Research studies have shown that those who progress better in learning turn out to have better self-awareness and better strategies for self-regulation than their slower learning peers (see, e.g., Brown and Ferrara 1985). Thus self-assessment becomes an important focus of assessment for learning. Peer-assessment also deserves priority, for it is by engaging in critical discussion of their work with their peers that learners are most likely to come to be objective about the strengths and weaknesses of their work. The main message is that students need to understand what it means to learn. They need to monitor how they go about planning and revising, to reflect on their learning, and to learn to determine for themselves if they understand. Such skills enhance metacognition, which is the essential strategic competence for learning.

When the teacher starts from where the learners are, helps them to take responsibility for their learning, and develops peer- and self-assessment to promote metacognition, the teacher becomes a supporter rather than a director of learning. This idea was taken further by Vygotsky (1962), who emphasized that because learning proceeds by an interaction between the teacher and the learner, the terms and conventions of the discourse are socially determined, and its effectiveness depends on the extent to which these terms and conventions are shared. His influence can be seen in the following statement:

> *Participation in social practice is a fundamental form of learning. Learning involves becoming attuned to the constraints and resources, the limits and possibilities, that are involved in the practices of the community. Learning is promoted by the social norms that value the search for understanding.*
> (Bransford, Brown, and Cocking 1999, xii)

Wood, Bruner, and Ross (1976) developed this approach by introducing the metaphor of "scaffolding"—the teacher provides the scaffold for the building, but the building itself can only be constructed by the learner. In this supportive role, the teacher has to discern the potential of the learner to advance in understanding, so that new challenges are neither too trivial nor too demanding. Vygotsky called the gap between what learners can do on their own and what they can do with the help of others the "zone of proximal development." One function of assessment is to help to identify this zone accurately and to explore progress within it.

All of this shows how important it is for the teacher to develop a classroom discourse through which all students learn to internalize and use the language and the norms of argument used by scientists to explain phenomena and to solve problems (Bransford, Brown, and Cocking 1999, 171–75). Thus, the way students talk about science, both in informal and formal terms, is important formative assessment material for teachers (Lemke 1990).

Because a learner's response will be sensitive to the language and social context of any communication, it follows that assessments, whether formative or summative, have to be very carefully framed, both in their language and context of presentation, if they are to avoid bias (i.e., unfair effects on those from particular gender, social, ethnic, or linguistic groups). The importance of context is also a far-reaching issue. For example, tests that ask questions about mathematics that might be used in society in general might be failed by a student who can use the same mathematics in a familiar school context, and vice versa (Boaler 2000).

The discussion in this section has been limited to the cognitive aspect of links between assessment and student response. Other important elements will be explored in the next section.

Assessment for Learning

In the broadest sense of the word, assessment is something that we do all the time. We encounter a new situation, make a judgment about the meaning of what is happening, and decide what to do next. The evidence of our encounters continually shapes and reshapes our actions. Our actions may be more effective if we are flexible—that is, if we are prepared to modify our intentions in the light of events. They might also be more effective if we probe the situation carefully in order to ensure that we understand what is going on before jumping to conclusions.

All of this applies in particular to life inside the classroom. The teacher has some understanding of the state of the students' learning, and must decide what to do next. This understanding is bound to be imperfect, but it can be refined by setting up activities through which the students will provide more evidence. So the cycle is to evoke or explore, to interpret the feedback, and then to modify the teaching actions.

The key to formative assessment lies in this flexibility—the capacity to change what was planned in order to meet the needs exposed by the evidence. The prospects are improved by finding ways to so elicit evidence that key features of the learning are illuminated; this can be called *assessment for learning*. However, there is little point in doing this if the evidence is not used to fashion what happens next; only when such refashioning occurs does the assessment become *formative assessment* (Black and Wiliam 1998). It is necessary to stress this feature; some teachers believe that they are engaged in formative assessment when, even though they are listening to their students, they then proceed with a lesson plan despite what they have heard.

The concept of assessment is a very general one—in the classroom it is happening all the time. When the looks on the faces of the students, or their written work, or their oral answers to a question are appraised, the teacher is assessing. A quiz or written test is also an occasion for assessment, but it is only one among many possibilities. As outlined above, the quality of the assessment feedback will depend on the quality of the interventions that evoke that feedback. It is here that the theories of learning become relevant. A question that asks about a technical term—for example, "What is the unit of current?"—serves a very different purpose from one that probes understanding—for example, "Does the current get used up as it goes through the light bulb?" The former question looks for recall, and there is little that can be done with the response apart from noting whether or not it is correct.

The latter question probes rather deeply, for it has a basis in research evidence that the notion of "current used up" is a common misconception. One way for a teacher to respond is to listen to an answer and then to tell the class the right answer; such action, however, is not responsive to the evidence. A second way is to explore opinions among a class to stimulate a discussion about the concept of current, which could lead to a test with a simple circuit with ammeters on either side of the bulb. This second way is formative, for it explores understanding, involves students actively in the learning process, and follows the learning principle that effective learning starts from where learners are and helps them to see the need to change. Furthermore, insofar as discussion is evoked, the learning is in the context of a discourse in a learning community rather than being a one-way transmission. Thus, there is an intimate connection between good formative assessment and the implementation in the classroom of sound principles of learning.

Similar arguments can be applied to other learning activities, notably the marking of written work, the use of peer- and self-assessment, the possibilities for the formative use of written tests, and so on. As teachers change to make formative assessment a constant feature of their work, they will inevitably be changing their roles as teachers. They have to be more interactive with their students, and they have to give them more responsibility for learning. This leads to a change in role, from directing students to empowering them (Black et al. 2002).

Assessment and the Student

Change in the role of teachers must lead, in the formative classroom, to changes in the roles of students. One type of change will be cognitive. As questions become more searching, and as the classroom routine is altered to depend more on the active involvement of the learner, students will find that they have to think more and take responsibility for doing more of the work themselves. Because formative work requires the elicitation of students' ideas, they will also have to be more willing to expose these ideas and to submit them to discussion and challenge by their peers as well as by their teachers. This calls for a change in the expectations of students, and such change may disconcert many, who are likely to resist. Thus it becomes important to build a supportive environment. Students must learn to listen to one another, to respect one another's opinions, and to understand that learning works through exploration and challenge, not by rewarding those who are right and labeling those who are wrong.

However, learning is not just a cognitive exercise—it involves the whole person. The need to motivate pupils is evident, but it is often assumed that motivation should consist of extrinsic rewards, such as merits, grades, gold stars, and prizes. Ample evidence challenges this assumption. If a learning exercise is seen as a competition, then everyone is aware that there will be losers as well as winners; those who have a track record as losers will see little point in trying. Thus, the problem is to motivate everyone, even though some are bound to achieve less than others. In tackling this problem, teachers need to realize that the type of feedback they give is very important. Many research studies support this assertion, as the following citations attest:

- Pupils told that feedback "will help you to learn" learn more than those told that "how you do tells us how smart you are and what grades you'll get"; the difference is greatest for low attainers (Newman and Schwager 1995).

- Those given marks as feedback are likely to see the marks as a way to compare themselves with others (ego-involvement); those given only comments see such feedback as helping them to improve (task-involvement). The latter group outperforms the former (Butler 1987).

- In a competitive system, low attainers attribute their performance to lack of "ability" and high attainers attribute their performance to effort. In a task-oriented system, all attribute their performance to effort, and learning is improved, particularly among low attainers (Craven, Marsh, and Debus 1991).

- A comprehensive review of research studies of feedback showed that feedback improved performance in 60 percent of the studies. In the cases where it was not helpful, the feedback turned out to be merely a judgment or grading with no indication of how to improve (Kluger and DeNisi 1996).

In general, feedback in the form of rewards or grades enhances ego rather than task involvement. It can focus pupils' attention on their "ability" rather than on the importance of effort, thereby damaging the self-esteem of low attainers and leading to problems of "learned helplessness" (Dweck 1986). Feedback that focuses on what needs to be done can encourage all students to believe that they can improve. Such feedback enhances learning, both directly through the effort that can ensue and indirectly by supporting the motivation to invest such effort.

Assessment across Subjects

Everyday assessment is not an abstract idea; it is a concrete activity that the science teacher conducts in and through the stuff of science education. While there are generic principles applicable to any learning, practical implementation is bound to be different in the teaching of science and the teaching of, say, history.

The formulation of insightful oral or written questions and the subsequent development of dialogue through which students become involved in their own learning are essential components of formative assessment. For example, a useful question about heat transfer can be based on a picture of three imaginary children arguing about the melting of a snowman. The scenario is that the sun is shining, and there is a breeze blowing, and child A suggests that they wrap a black coat around their snowman to stop the sun from melting it. Child B objects that the black coat will warm up the snowman, and child C says that it all depends on the wind. The class can be asked to say what they think about the arguments of these three children. The question is conceptually rich in that it can be used to open up discussion of radiation, conduction, and convection. But it has two other features. One is that it has the potential to elicit a well-known misconception—namely, that a coat actively warms you up rather than reducing the outward flow of heat. The second feature of the question is that it is likely to interest the children because it uses a context, and a practical need for decision, with which they might identify. Such knowledge, about the way children might think and might be interested, is called *pedagogical content knowledge*. Science teachers can only plan and conduct an exercise of this type on the basis of understanding of the concepts involved and of the relevant pedagogical content knowledge.

In this snowman example, there is a set of "correct" ideas and a "right answer," albeit a complex one. More generally, there is in any intellectual discipline a spectrum of possible issues, with those issues having well-defined answers lying at one end and those with a variety of good answers lying at the other. Emphasis on inquiry works at the latter end. It calls for a pedagogy that promotes investigations in which students have to exercise initiative and follow a variety of paths and for which the criteria of achievement are concerned with the quality of strategies and arguments rather than with attainment of a single, well-defined outcome. The type of formative "scaffolding" needed here is more akin to that of the teacher of English who is helping students to develop their individual writing styles than to that of the same teacher concerned with basic rules of punctuation.

The current trend of reform in science education is to shift the balance of learning toward the open-ended. This calls for emphasis on inquiry skills, but there is a further and broader aim, which is to engage students in discussion of the effects of the advances of science on society, issues that are, or ought to be, of evident importance to them. Such issues are almost always areas of controversy. A discussion of, say, genetic variation might start with clarification of the concepts, but will change style when the discussion moves on to whether to develop genetically modified crops and the sale of genetically modified foods. What matters here is the quality of the arguments that are deployed, and the teacher has to guide students, in the midst of controversy, both to argue and to listen carefully (Osborne 2000). Teachers in the social sciences might be more experienced in such work than their science colleagues.

Teachers have to be flexible in varying their classroom styles to promote different types of learning. Indeed, many science teachers who are accustomed to dealing with "fixed-answer" topics find it very hard to cope with discussions for which the aim is to help learners be critical about the quality of the arguments, rather than about the correctness of the outcome. The shift from "delivery" modes of learning to interactive modes is an essential step in developing this flexibility. As hinted above, science teachers struggling with the new challenges presented by the standards reforms might find help through study of the classroom practices of colleagues who teach other subjects.

Summary of the Issues

Two main themes emerge from this chapter. The first is that tensions and synergies exist between different purposes of assessment, raising problems for both policy makers and classroom teachers. It is obvious that insofar as there is tension, priority must be given to assessment for learning—the measurement of the outcome of schooling can hardly be more important than the means to secure that outcome.

If this is accepted, then all concerned must find ways to achieve a new equilibrium between the formative and summative purposes, which involves finding ways in which summative systems can serve rather than damage good learning. One obstacle to such achievement has been revealed by many surveys of teachers' classroom practices, for these have shown that assessment practices are one of the weakest aspects of many teachers' work. In part this may well be due to the dominance of summative tests, which provide many teachers with models for assessment—models that are unhelpful because they are not designed as aids to everyday learning.

So there is a need to reconstruct, to build up, everyday assessment so that it serves its first purpose—to elicit and to serve the needs of each learner. A secondary reason why such a development is of central importance is that only when teachers are more skilled and more confident in their own assessment practices might it be possible for them to command the public confidence that is needed so that they can play a strong part in any reconstruction of assessment and testing as a whole.

The second theme of this chapter is the necessity for reform of the classroom as a learning environment. Four principles have been set out for the design of learning environments (Bransford, Brown, and Cocking 1999, xvi–xvii): They should be *learner-centered, knowledge-centered, community-centered,* and strong in *assessment for learning.* To create a *learner-centered* environment, the teacher must start from where the learner is and work by interaction and formative feedback to promote learning. Teachers must also attend to the learners' understanding of how they can learn and the learners' confidence that they can all learn.

For a school environment to be *knowledge-centered*, the focus has to be on a coherent approach to developing important knowledge and skills, an approach in which all students can grasp what the purposes and values of science are and can feel that they are actually taking part, albeit in a modest way, in sharing in the practices of scientists. So active participation of all is clearly essential.

To be *community-centered*, the environment must again be one in which active participation by everyone in the serious business of learning about science is a priority. Through lively discourse in the classroom, the understanding of all students is advanced and refined and their power to participate in scientific argument is developed. The dominance of competition through testing, which creates winners and losers, and of labeling pupils as "bright" or "dull," ought to be replaced by a shared belief that all students can make progress—and can help one another to do so, as well.

Formative assessment is an essential ingredient for each of these aspects of a learning environment.

References

Baxter, G. P., and R. J. Shavelson. 1994. Science performance assessments: Benchmarks and surrogates. *International Journal of Educational Research* 21: 279–98.

Black, P. J. 1990. APU science: The past and the future. *School Science Review* 72 (258): 13–28.

Black, P., and D. Wiliam. 1998. Inside the black box: Raising standards through classroom assessment. *Phi Delta Kappan* 80 (2): 139–48.

Black, P., C. Harrison, C. Lee, B. Marshall, and D. Wiliam. 2002. *Working inside the black box: Assessment for learning in the classroom.* London, UK: King's College London, Department of Education and Professional Studies.

Boaler, J. 2000. Introduction: Intricacies of knowledge, practice and theory. In *Multiple perspectives on mathematics teaching and learning*, ed. J. Boaler, 1–17. Westport, NJ: Ablex.

Bransford, J. A., A. Brown, and R. Cocking. 1999. *How people learn: Brain, mind, experience and school.* Washington, DC: National Academy Press.

Brown, A. L., and R. A. Ferrara.1985. Diagnosing zones of proximal development. In *Culture, communication and cognition: Vygotskian perspectives,* ed. J. V. Wersch, 273 305. Cambridge: Cambridge University Press.

Butler, R. 1987. Task-involving and ego-involving properties of evaluation: Effects of different feedback conditions on motivational perceptions, interest and performance. *Journal of Educational Psychology* 79 (4): 474–82.

Collins, A. 2002. How students learn and how teachers teach. In *Learning science and the science of learning*, ed. R. W. Bybee, 3–11. Arlington, VA: National Science Teachers Association.

Craven, R. G., H. W. Marsh, and R. L. Debus. 1991. Effects of internally focused feedback on enhancement of academic self-concept. *Journal of Educational Psychology* 83 (1): 17–27.

Dweck, C. S. 1986. Motivational processes affecting learning. *American Psychologist (Special Issue: Psychological science and education)* 41 (10): 1040–1048.

Kluger, A. N., and A. DeNisi. 1996. The effects of feedback interventions on performance: A historical review, a meta-analysis, and a preliminary feedback intervention theory. *Psychological Bulletin* 119 (2): 254–84.

Lemke, J. L. 1990. *Talking science: Language, learning and values.* Norwood, NJ: Ablex.

Linn, R. L. 2000. Assessments and accountability. *Educational Researcher* 29 (2): 4–14.

Messick, S. 1989. Validity. In *Educational Measurement* (3rd ed.), ed. R. L. Linn, 13–103. London: Macmillan.

Newman, R. S., and M. T. Schwager. 1995. Students' help seeking during problem solving: Effects of grade, goal, and prior achievement. *American Educational Research Journal* 32 (2): 352–76.

Osborne, J. 2000. Science for citizenship. In *Good practice in science teaching: What research has to say,* eds. M. Monk and J. Osborne, 225–40. Philadelphia, PA: Open University Press.

Shepard, L. A. 1992. Commentary: What policy makers who mandate tests should know about the new psychology of intellectual ability and learning. In *Changing assessments: Alternative views of aptitude, achievement and instruction*, eds. B. R. Gifford and M. C. O'Connor, 301–28. Boston and Dordrecht: Kluwer.

Vygotsky, L. S.1962. *Thought and language.* New York: Wiley.

Wood, D. 1998. *How children think and learn: The social contexts of cognitive development* (2nd ed.). Oxford: Blackwell.

Wood, D., J. S. Bruner, and G. Ross. 1976. The role of tutoring in problem solving. *Journal of Child Psychology and Psychiatry* 17: 89–100.

Learning through Assessment: Assessment *for* Learning in the Science Classroom[1]

Anne Davies

Anne Davies has taught both elementary- and university-level students and has worked as a school administrator and a district consultant. Currently, she is involved in research projects; is preparing a facilitator's guide to her book *Making Classroom Assessment Work* (Merville, BC: Connections Publishing, 2000); and is conducting workshops and teaching graduate courses internationally. She has been a recipient of the Hilroy Fellowship for Innovative Teaching as well as a Social Sciences and Humanities Council doctoral fellowship.

A classroom assessment process that supports student learning is made up of three general parts. First, teachers review the curriculum and standards documents and summarize in their own words the learning that students are expected to accomplish. They collect and review samples and models that show what the learning looks like for students of a particular age range, and they think through what kinds of evidence their students could produce to show they have learned what they needed to learn. This summary guides their work with students and helps them articulate the learning destination clearly and simply to others.

Once the big picture is established, the second task is for teachers to work with students to bring them into the assessment process. They do this by talking about the learning, showing samples and discussing what the evidence might look like, setting criteria with students, asking them to self-assess, and giving them time to learn.

Third, as students become involved in assessment *for* learning, they learn to become partners in a continuous assessment cycle that supports their learning. In this cycle, students receive and give themselves descriptive feedback as they learn in relation to the criteria. From time to time they discuss their own learning in relation to what needs to be learned, they self-assess, and set goals. They revisit and reset the criteria as they learn more. They collect evidence of learning, present their evidence to others, and receive feedback. This leads to more self-assessing, goal setting, and learning.

Seeing It Work

What does this process look like in a middle school science classroom? The rest of this chapter presents an example of assessment that leads to learning. In this example, students are learning how to collect evidence as part of a scientific research project in their area.[2]

---

[1] Copyright © 2003 by the National Science Teachers Association and Anne Davies. This chapter is adapted from Chapter 1 in A. Davies. 2000. *Making classroom assessment work*. Merville, BC: Connections Publishing.

[2] My thanks to Debbie Jamieson, Pembroke School, Pembroke, Maine, for providing this example from her classroom.

Talking about the Learning

"Our class has been asked to help with an international environmental problem. The problem is an invasion of green crabs. Have you noticed them at the beaches? People around North America are watching and tracking the invasion, trying to figure out the impact on local species, finding ways to minimize the impact, and helping to identify possible solutions in advance of their arrival elsewhere. Our class can help. It will mean spending time at the beach collecting evidence and reporting on the impact here in our coastal areas. Are you interested in becoming involved? There is a website devoted to this project. Let's go online and look at the data being collected, what people are learning, and how we can help."

When students engage in conversation before any learning activity or task, the talk clarifies options, highlights possible plans, and encourages sharing of information. As students work with teachers to define what learning is and what it looks like, they shift from being passive learners to being actively involved in their own learning. By being engaged, they use and build neural pathways in their brains. This means they are more likely to be able to access their learning easily and for a longer period of time—way beyond the end of the unit or test.

Relevance is key to student learning. Why bother? Is it worth it? Does it count? These are questions students ask as they are trying to figure out whether to commit to learning. When students and teachers talk about why the learning is relevant to students' lives, students begin to understand more fully what needs to be learned.

When students are in partnership with teachers and others in support of learning, more learning is possible because learning is socially mediated (Vygotsky 1978). Berger and Luckman (1967, 3) explain: "All human knowledge is developed, transmitted, and maintained in social situations." Talking about the learning provides an opportunity for collaborative feedback—from student and teacher perspectives. What was learned? What evidence is there? What worked? What didn't? What might be done differently next time?

Showing Samples

"I'm really glad you are interested in becoming part of this project. As we gather evidence about the green crabs it will be really important that we do it properly so the data can be collated across research sites. Did anyone notice what kind of data was being reported? What do you think we will need to collect?"

When we give students samples to review and when we talk with them about what is important in their learning, we help them build mental models of what success looks like. When teachers spend time with students, sharing samples as well as connecting what students already know to what they need to know, students' understanding of what they will be learning and of what will be assessed increases. When we involve students in this way, they use their prior knowledge and learn more about the language of learning and assessment.

Before teachers show samples of student work that illustrate learning destinations, they should decide on the purpose for the learning. For example:

1. *Do you want all students to do the same thing in the same way?* In collecting scientific evidence there is a quality standard that needs to be adhered to. The samples need to help students understand exactly what quality looks like. There may be specific scientific criteria to demonstrate.

2. *Do you want students to show what they know in a variety of ways?* Teachers can provide numerous samples that help students understand the range of what is possible. This open-ended destination supports "all kinds of minds."

3. *Do you want students to show individual progress over time?* Does quality have many different looks or just one? When teachers know that different students are at different points in their development, they can use samples that show a range of what the learning looks like over time. In this case, samples become a kind of road map of quality on the journey to learning.

Samples are particularly important for the students who struggle the most in our classrooms. When samples represent work that is too far away from what students know and are able to do, students cannot see how to get from where they are to where they need to be. If samples are limited to showing what students already know and can do, they fail to orient students toward what they need to know next. Selecting samples needs to be a process that is carefully linked to the purpose of the learning and the learning needs of students. When we use samples to illustrate the learning destination, more students are able to participate in setting criteria, in giving themselves feedback, and in assessing their own way to quality and success.

Setting and Using Criteria

"Our collected data is important to the success of this project. I want you to think about what is important as you collect the data about the green crabs. Let's brainstorm a list. What's important when we are collecting?" [Students call out their ideas, and Ms. J. takes notes on the board until their ideas run out.]

Make sure you have the right species.

Count more than once to make sure.

Count the green crabs.

Measure the square on the beach.

Be accurate when counting.

Count EVERY species in that area (even the barnacles!).

Survey all the animals in different spots.

Be exact about everything.

"I think that is a really good beginning. Different projects require different kinds of data. Dr. R. is coming this afternoon. She is the local project coordinator from the university. We will ask her what else is important as we collect the data."

Some of our students know what teachers want without it ever being made explicit. Some students simply don't get it or have expectations and perceptions embedded in their personal backgrounds (perhaps culture and family experience) that do not match those a teacher may assume are understood by all students (Busick 2001; Delpit 1995). When we make the criteria explicit, share the process of learning with each other, and assess (give descriptive feedback) according to the agreed criteria, we give more students the opportunity to learn. We begin to make more of the implicit expectations explicit.

Giving students time to discover what they already know, what they are learning, and what they can learn from each other provides a scaffold for future learning. Knowing what they are learning, the varied looks it can have, and what the desired level of performance looks like gives students the information they need to assess themselves as they learn—to keep themselves on track. Setting criteria with students helps teachers know more about students' prior knowledge as well as giving students the language needed to self-monitor progress.

When criteria for success are set with learners, they can check their thinking and performance and develop deeper understandings. Perhaps most significantly, students' expectations of themselves and their beliefs in what they are capable of accomplishing increase dramatically. Using criteria or creating rubrics that describe levels of quality in relation to criteria, samples, or models results in more learning. Simply put, students' involvement in establishing and using performance criteria teaches them what "good work" is, what it looks like, and how to produce and distinguish it.

Self-Assessing and Goal Setting

"Now that we are back from the beach and our first data collection, I want you to review the criteria for collecting data that we created and think about what you did that helped you to be successful and what you need to do

differently next time. Record your ideas. Here are two different procedures. Choose one."

Procedure #1:
Complete the following—

Here is a sample of the data I collected:

One thing that worked was ...

One thing that didn't work was ...

One thing I might do differently next time is ...

Procedure #2:
Take your copy of the criteria and use a highlighter pen to note the things you did that worked and in another color one thing you need to do differently next time. Select a sample of your collected data to show evidence of your work. When you are finished, compare your ideas with your partner.

When we think about what we've done, we may come to understand it in a different way. Self-assessment gives learners the opportunity to think about their thinking and their learning—a process called *metacognition.* Michael Fullan puts it this way: "An event is not an experience until you reflect upon it." When students and teachers self-assess, they confirm, consolidate, and integrate new knowledge.

Students, through the "assessment conversation," help other students in the class learn. When students are engaged in discussion with teachers about the learning expected before any learning activity or task, the talk clarifies options, highlights possible plans, and encourages sharing of information. Knowing what they are learning and what it looks like gives students the information they need.

When conversations about learning take place in the group, learners can check their thinking and performance, develop deeper understandings of their learning, and become more strategic in their planning and monitoring. Researchers studying the role of emotions and the brain say that experiences such as these prepare learners to take the risks necessary for learning.

Revisiting Criteria

"As you were reviewing the criteria and thinking about collecting data, was there something you did that worked that isn't on the criteria sheet? What do we need to add to the criteria for collecting data now that we've collected some data about the green crabs?"

As students learn and assess, they define and redefine the criteria with teachers, each time trying to make them more specific and accurate. When students are involved, criteria become more specific as they learn more about high-quality work. The source of ideas for criteria may come from anywhere—hands-on learning experiences, classroom lessons, or experiences outside the classroom. The important thing is that student learning is acknowledged and that the criteria continue to change as students learn more. Like samples, criteria vary to reflect the learning journey and destination. Consider the following purposes:

1. *Do you want all students to do the same thing in the same way?* For example, in the case of collecting scientific evidence there is a quality standard that needs to be adhered to. In this case the criteria need to describe that quality standard. It would be inappropriate to aim for anything less.

2. *Do you want students to show what they know in a variety of ways?* For example, students may choose a different way to express what was learned. It doesn't matter how the information is presented, but accuracy should not be sacrificed.

3. *Do you want students to show individual progress over time?* Does quality have many different looks or just one? For example, if the focus of the criteria was searching for and analyzing information, there may be an acceptable range. In this case a rubric describing development may be helpful.

Criteria can become a rubric when different levels of development, quality, or achievement over time are described. Rubrics that support student learning

- describe what students do at each level of quality or performance,

- are written in simple, clear language that students can understand,

- provide information about incremental steps students can take that will lead to greater success, and

- focus on what the student needs to do to be more successful.

For example, the preferred description would state, "needs complete ideas, needs more details" rather than "incomplete ideas, lack of detail." The former description helps students understand what to do next time. It is an example of assessment *for* learning. The latter description merely judges the work and does not give students information they can use to improve performance. It is an example of assessment *of* learning. If the rubric you are considering using describes ways students can completely miss the learning destination, consider modifying it so it supports learning.

Providing Specific, Descriptive Feedback

"When you're finished talking with your partner, please hand in your science notebooks, open to some of the evidence you've collected, and attach your self-assessment. I am going to review your work thus far and give you feedback."

Specific, descriptive feedback is essential for learning (Hattie in press; Sadler 1989; Senge 1990; Shepard 2000; Stiggins 1996; Sylwester 1995). Descriptive feedback serves three goals: (1) it describes strengths on which a student can build; (2) it articulates the manner in which performance falls short of desired criteria with an eye to suggesting how that can be improved; and (3) it gives information that enables the learner to adjust what he or she is doing in order to get better. Specific, descriptive feedback that focuses on what was done successfully and points the way to improvement has a positive effect on learning.

Evaluative feedback, particularly summary feedback, is very different. It tells the learner how she or he has performed as compared to others or to some standard. Evaluative feedback is highly reduced, often communicated using letters, numbers, checks, or other symbols. It is encoded. This creates problems for students—particularly for students who are struggling. Summary feedback does not address students' needs or the manner in which further growth and development can be realized and may affect students' motivation to learn. Students with poor marks are more likely to see themselves as failures. Students who see themselves as failures may be less motivated, and therefore less likely to succeed as learners, than their peers with high marks.

If we evaluate too early, we limit descriptive feedback and risk interrupting the learning. When we assess during the learning and evaluate at the end of the learning, we give students time to practice and learn before we judge the evidence.

Setting Goals

"Before we go to the beach for today's data collection, I want you to review your notes from last time about what worked and what didn't when we were down there last collecting data. Given our experiences last time collecting data, can we make a list of advice we would give other students doing similar work? I'll record your ideas. [Teacher writes down ideas for everyone to see.] *Before we go to the beach, write down one idea you are going to use to make your data collection better this time. Write it at the top of your data collection sheet. When we return, you will need to show evidence that you tried to improve your data collection using the idea you have selected."*

When students work together to set criteria, self-assess, and reset criteria, they come to understand the process of assessment and begin to learn the language of assessment. Students gain a clear picture of what they need to learn and where they are in relation to where they need to be, and they get an opportunity to begin to identify possible next steps in their learning. Research indicates that closing in on a goal triggers a part of the brain linked to motivation (e.g., Csikszentmihalyi 1990; Pert 1997; Pinker 1997). Setting goals is a powerful way to focus students' learning.

Students involved in self-assessment and goal setting in relation to criteria learn more. When students self-assess, they gain insights about their learning that help them learn. These insights help them monitor their learning and provide practice in giving themselves descriptive feedback. When student self-assessments are shared with teachers, teachers gain a better understanding about where students are in relation to where they need to be. When students share their thinking with teachers, teachers can teach better.

Doing things more than once is essential for learning. In education we tend to jump on one bandwagon and then jump on the next one to come along. We would learn more as a profession if we just stuck to one thing and learned how to do it well. The same is true for our students. It is when they do something the second and third time that they learn what they know and what they need to know. Students need practice time to learn. It is when students practice that they are able to take what they are learning and apply it at deeper and deeper levels.

Collecting Evidence of Learning

"Congratulations. Our first data collection is over. The data have been submitted. We will be doing this again in the spring. We have made our report to the local environmental group. They were very impressed. They got some important information. They also have some ideas for us to improve our data collection next time. Also the new video camera will help us record more evidence. Now that we are finished this first part of the project, I want you to collect evidence that you have learned to show your parents at the end of term. Remember our criteria. What evidence do you have that shows you have met the criteria in a quality fashion? Who has some ideas about what that evidence might include?"

Until recently, classroom assessment information—evidence of learning—referred exclusively to traditional paper and pencil tests. Such classroom tests can measure some kinds of learning; they cannot measure all the knowledge, abilities, and skills students are responsible for learning. Because learning is more than recitation, assessment is more than recall tasks. Assessment evidence is more than tests; it includes a range of physical evidence as well as observations and conversations with learners about the learning. One way classroom assessment can be usefully understood is as a particular kind of classroom research that adapts research methods from anthropology and the human sciences. It is research into what students know and can do, their strengths and areas of need.

This involves gathering evidence of learning from a variety of sources over time and looking for patterns and trends. Such information gathering is one way to increase the reliability and validity of classroom assessment findings. This process has a history of use in the social sciences and is called *triangulation*. As students learn, there are three ways to acquire evidence of learning:

1. *Collecting products,* including tests, assignments, students' writings, projects, notebooks, constructions, images, demonstrations, and video- and audiotapes.

2. *Observing the process of learning,* including observation notes regarding hands-on, minds-on learning activities as well as learning journals and performances of various kinds across all subject areas.

3. *Communicating with students about their learning,* including conferences, reading written self-assessments, and interviews.

Collecting products, observing the process of learning, and communicating with students will provide a considerable range of evidence over time. This not only increases the potential for instructionally relevant insights into learning, it also provides for more accurate assessment of learning and therefore enhances the reliability and validity of the evidence thus assembled. Collections of student work—evidence of learning—may include anything that is relevant to learning and may vary from student to student. Collecting the same information from all students may not be fair and equitable because students show what they know in different ways. Allowing for a range of evidence encourages students to represent what they know in a variety of ways and gives teachers a way to fairly and more completely assess the learning.

Communicating Using Evidence of Learning

"Today your parents and other invited guests will be viewing the data we collected concerning the invasion of the green crabs as well as looking at your individual collections of evidence for this project and for science in general this term. You have all worked hard. What do you want people to notice about your work? What kind of feedback do you want to ask for from people who see your work? Could you please fill in a 'Please notice ...' card for your work? Would you like to ask people to fill in a comment card telling you what they liked and one suggestion they might have for next time?"

When we give students a chance to share their knowledge with each other and with us, they learn and we learn. Celebrating our accomplishments by sharing our work with others is part of the process of learning. The audience can be other people in the class, other classes, parents and guardians, or community members. When the learning is captured in print, on videotape, audiotape, or electronically, it becomes concrete evidence of learning.

Acknowledging our accomplishments by sharing our work with others extends the learning. When students are invited (and assisted) to collect and organize evidence of learning for the purpose of sharing that with others, they learn about

- what they have learned,

- what they need to learn, and

- what kind of support may be available and necessary to them to extend their learning.

It seems the presence of others influences what we attend to and what we know, and forces us to step back and reflect—to think about and assess what we're doing. When students reveal evidence of their learning to an audience (e.g., peers, teachers, parents), the students receive feedback and recognition from themselves and from others. When learners talk about their learning to people whose opinion they value, they learn more and are more likely to become resilient learners.

Students can use their collections of evidence of learning and portfolios to communicate in a variety of settings, including

- student-teacher conferences, in which students meet with teachers to present evidence of their learning and the conversation is between teacher and student in relation to the course goals;

- student-parent conferences that involve students and parents who meet at school or at home to review collections of evidence of learning that show growth or learning over time;

- student-parent-teacher conferences that complement written reports; and

- formal conference settings or exhibitions where students present evidence of learning and answer questions from a panel of community members, parents, and peers.

All of these ways of communicating have one thing in common: The student is actively involved in presenting a range of evidence of learning. The teacher assists by providing information regarding criteria and evidence of quality. Sometimes this is done through using samples that reflect a continuum of learning over time. These samples provide a reference point for conversation about student development and achievement. Teachers use samples of work that represent levels of quality to show parents where the student is in relation to the expected standard. This helps the teacher respond to the question many parents ask: "How is my child doing compared to the other students?" In a "verbal report card," parents are involved participants in understanding the evidence and in the "reporting" on the child's strengths, areas needing improvement, and the setting of goals.

Continuing the Learning

"This is the last time this year we will be collecting data on the green crabs on our beaches. Before we collect our data and prepare our report, I want to revisit our criteria and identify previous work we have done that meets or exceeds the criteria. Look at the criteria we set. Who has evidence from last time that illustrates what quality looks like? What other kind of evidence could prove you have met the criteria? You need to show what you've learned. You do that when you provide evidence that you have met, to a high degree of quality, each part of the criteria."

When students are involved in the assessment process they are motivated to learn. They learn how to think about their learning and how to self-assess—key aspects of metacognition. Also, when students are involved in assessment they have opportunities to share their learning with others whose opinions they care about. An audience gives purpose and creates a sense of responsibility for the learning. This increases the authenticity of the task.

In summary, students need to be involved in the classroom assessment process for the following reasons:

- Learners construct their own understandings. Therefore, learning how to learn—becoming an independent, self-directed, lifelong learner—involves learning how to assess and learning to use assessment information and insights to adjust learning behaviors and improve performance.

- Students' sense of quality in performance and expectations of their own performance are increased as a result of their engagement in the assessment process.

- Students can create more comprehensive collections of evidence to demonstrate their learning because they know and can represent what they've learned in various ways to serve various purposes.

- The validity and reliability of classroom assessment are increased when students are involved in collecting evidence of learning. Also, the collections are likely to be more complete and comprehensive than if teachers alone collect evidence of learning.

Assessment *for* Learning in the Science Classroom

"Remember that the person doing the work is the one growing the dendrites," writes Pat Wolfe (2001, 187). The assessment for learning process described in this chapter can be overwhelming if teachers believe it is their job to do all the work. Teachers who understand assessment *for* learning are shifting more and more of the responsibility for learning and assessment to students. This process can be a slow one as students learn how to learn by becoming fully involved in the assessment process. What does it look like when it happens? Students, in partnership with teachers,

- are able to articulate the learning destination,

- collect and refer to samples that show quality work,

- are able to describe what evidence of learning might look like,

- set criteria defining quality,

- have time to learn,

- receive and give themselves specific, descriptive feedback as they learn,

- debrief their learning with their peers and others,

- self-assess and set goals,

- revisit and reset the criteria as they learn more,

- collect evidence of their own learning, and

- present their evidence of learning to others and receive feedback.

Classroom teachers will know they are well on their way to assessment *for* learning when they can state, "I involve students in ongoing assessment for learning. I summarize in my own words the learning that students are expected to accomplish. I collect and review samples and models to show what the learning looks like for students of a particular age range. I think about what kinds of evidence students could produce to show they have learned what they needed to learn. I ensure that the evidence of learning is valid and reliable by using the process of triangulation. I collect evidence over time so emerging trends and patterns can be identified. I use classroom assessment information to fine-tune instruction and the learning environment. Students are fully involved in the assessment process. They are working harder than I am and learning more than ever before."

References

Berger, P. L., and T. Luckman. 1967. *The social construction of reality*. Garden City, NY: Anchor Books.

Busick, K. Conversation with author, Kaneohe, HI, 2001.

Csikszentmihalyi, M. 1990. *Flow: The psychology of optimal experience*. New York: Harper and Row.

Davies, A. 2000. *Making classroom assessment work*. Merville, BC: Connections Publishing.

Delpit, L. 1995. *Other people's children: Cultural conflict in the classroom*. New York: New Press.

Hattie, J. In press. *The power of feedback for enhancing learning*. Auckland, NZ: University of Auckland.

Pert, C. 1997. *Molecules of emotion: Why you feel the way you feel*. New York: Simon and Schuster.

Pinker, S. 1997. *How the mind works*. New York: Harper Collins.

Sadler, R. 1989. Formative assessment and the design of instructional systems. *Instructional Science* 18: 119–44.

Senge, P. M. 1990. *The fifth discipline: The art and practice of the learning organization*. New York: Doubleday.

Shepard, L. 2000. The role of assessment in a learning culture. *Educational Researcher* 29 (7): 4–14.

Stiggins R. 1996. Remarks made during keynote presentation, Assessment Training Institute Annual Conference, Portland, OR.

Sylwester, R. 1995. *A celebration of neurons: An educator's guide to the brain*. Alexandria, VA: Association for Supervision and Curriculum Development.

Vygotsky, L. S. 1978. *Mind in society: The development of higher psychological processes*, eds. M. Cole, V. John-Steiner, S. Scribner, and E. Souberman. Cambridge, MA: Harvard University Press.

Wolfe, P. 2001. *Brain matters: Translating research into classroom practice*. Alexandria, VA: Association for Supervision and Curriculum Development.

Examining Students' Work

Cary I. Sneider

Cary I. Sneider is vice president for programs at the Museum of Science in Boston, where he oversees live programming for approximately 1.6 million visitors each year. In addition to his work at the museum, he is currently chair of the Committee on Science Education K–12 at the Center for Education, National Research Council. Cary has taught science in grades 5–12 in Massachusetts, Maine, California, Costa Rica, and Micronesia. He received a teaching certificate and Ph.D. in science education from the University of California at Berkeley. His research interests have focused on helping students unravel their misconceptions in science and on new ways to link science centers and schools to promote student inquiry. His publications include K–12 teachers' guides, articles about the instructional uses of computers, and research studies on how children learn science. He helped to develop the National Science Education Standards (NRC 1996) and contributed to *Designing Professional Development for Teachers of Mathematics and Science* (Loucks-Horsley et al. 1998). In 1997 he received the NSTA Distinguished Informal Science Education award.

I have been fortunate to teach science in a wide variety of situations, and I've learned a great deal from each of them. In this chapter I'll share some of those experiences, with particular reference to what I've learned from examining students' work. I'll begin with my first teaching experience, as a tutor at an Upward Bound summer program in Cambridge, Massachusetts.

Learning to Teach

My assignment that summer was teaching high school math to a group of about ten sophomores. I chose a topic that the students would be likely to encounter in the following school year—trigonometric functions. I approached the teaching of mathematics through induction. I wanted my students to "discover" the trigonometric functions by measuring the edges of right triangles and taking ratios. So, I assigned the students the task of constructing several similar right triangles and dividing the length of the opposite side by the adjacent side (the tangent). I expected the answers to vary somewhat due to inaccuracies in measurement, but for the ratios to be approximately the same. Then I'd assign them to construct several more similar right triangles, but with a different angle, and so on, until they had constructed a rough table of tangents.

The lesson was planned beautifully. I expected the students to go on to learn about the sine and cosine functions, then to apply the tables they constructed to word problems. So, when the students encountered these functions in school, they would understand how the tables of trigonometric functions were derived and would soon master the subject.

That was when I learned that lessons never go as planned. The students were able to construct triangles and take the ratios of the sides, but their answers for several similar triangles were wildly different! I could see the problem when I walked around the room and looked carefully at what they had done. They were all using their protractors in different ways. Apparently, the students had not been taught (or did not remember) how to use a protractor. I changed the objective of the lesson from teaching about tangents to teaching about protractors; for many of the students, a lesson about how angles were measured in degrees was also necessary. In an approach that many science teachers know all too well, I had to "back up" to where my students were before I could progress to the original learning objective.

We eventually did get around to creating a rough table of tangents for 10° intervals, but we never would have arrived at that point if I had not been able to see how they were holding their protractors. I had previously thought hands-on activities represented an important way for students to learn concepts and skills. While that may be true, the valuable insight I gained was that hands-on activities also allowed me to see how my students were thinking—and that was absolutely essential if I was to adjust my teaching objectives to suit their needs. In brief, I learned two important things about assessment from my first teaching experience:

Insight #1 We need to be prepared to modify not only our approach, but also our teaching objectives in response to feedback on student thinking.

Insight #2 Hands-on activities provide opportunities for us to see what our students are thinking.

How Directive Should We Be?

My third insight about examining student work came during my first full-time position in rural Maine. My high school teaching assignment included two sections of physics for seniors and three sections of general science for freshmen, as well as being the adviser to the student council and band. I quickly learned that as band director I needed to be in charge. The drum section simply could not be allowed to move faster than the woodwinds. But as a science teacher, taking charge was often counterproductive.

I was on fairly firm ground with the senior physics classes since I had the opportunity to use the Harvard Project Physics program. When I lectured and stopped to ask questions I could find out what one or two students were thinking, but it was not possible to find out what the rest of the students were thinking with Q&A alone. However, there were many lab activities that enabled me to engage my students' thinking so that I could work with them in small groups. Since I was not pressured to finish the text, I assigned many of the labs twice. The first time the students completed the lab as prescribed. The second time involved an original application of the concepts and tools.

For instance, to study motion we used Polaroid cameras and stroboscopes as well as some old ticker-tape timers that I dug out of the stockroom. In round one the students experimented with dynamics carts to measure and graph uniform and accelerated motion. In round two they selected some other motion to study. Balls thrown into the air, model rockets, and a good strong punch stand out in my mind as the motions they chose to study. Perhaps the most interesting was a windup baby doll that crawled along the floor. To study the motion of the doll, the students used a ticker-tape timer, which imprints a dot on a strip of paper every sixtieth of a second. The students taped one end of the paper strip to the doll and turned on the timer. On the strip of paper they saw a complex cyclic pattern of dots, in some places getting further apart (acceleration) and in other places closer together (deceleration). Listening to the students interpret a graph of these patterns was far more revealing of their understanding of motion than their work with the dynamics carts alone. I realized that by allowing the students some room for creativity, they became more deeply engaged in the project and it was easier for me to evaluate what they had learned and what they still found confusing (Sneider 1972).

There is a paradox here that's worth pointing out. On the one hand, as teachers we are encouraged to treat each student fairly in evaluating his or her work. That means we should ask all students the same questions and evaluate their performances by the same set of rules. That is why teachers give all of their students the same test at the end of a unit, and it is why school districts and states use standardized tests to measure success districtwide. On the other hand, such tests leave virtually no room for creativity, so we may not be seeing what students can do when motivated by their own curiosity. The paradox is resolved if we use creative problem-solving for the purpose of providing direct feedback to individuals and teams and modify instruction accordingly. As discussed in other chapters of this book, records of creative student work can be evaluated with the use of a rubric and therefore contribute to grades, but using such data for accountability of schools and teachers may be problematic. The main point here is that creative tasks provide invaluable opportunities to examine student thinking, and they should not be neglected in an effort to use assessment data for too many different purposes.

Insight #3 We should provide activities for students to apply what they have learned in new situations that allow some free choice or creativity.

The Importance of Listening

My major challenge during that first year of full-time teaching was the general science classes for freshmen. Since I was teaching with a provisional credential, I had virtually no experience in the instructional materials that were just then being developed with National Science Foundation support. And the textbooks that were available were hopelessly out of date. After floundering for a while, I settled on a method of teaching that provided even more insight into how my students' thinking evolved over time. It involved laboratory and discussion components in which I played the role of listener and coach rather than leader.

The labs all started with an open-ended challenge. "Find out all you can about falling objects, and make a list of what you discover." Or, "Explore shadows and make a list of what you find out." The students worked in lab groups of three or four students per team. I gathered materials and suggested ways for the students to explore these phenomena and helped them articulate their findings in writing, using large sheets of butcher paper. Then, the students sat in a large circle and discussed each other's lists, one statement at a time. I explained that the purpose of the discussion was to (1) understand the phenomenon that was being described; (2) determine if it was consistent with what they had experienced; (3) look at additional evidence if necessary; (4) modify the written statement if needed to be accurate; and (5) vote on whether or not they thought the statement was true as finally worded. If a large majority of the students agreed, we would call it a "natural law." We called these discussions "scientific conventions." Various students facilitated, so that I could sit on the side taking notes and acting as coach. The discussions were absolutely fascinating and sometimes quite surprising. For example, one topic the students investigated was "wave motion," including waves traveling in springs and ripple tanks. In the following transcription of a tape recording, the students are trying to decide among several statements to determine which best explains what occurs when a wave hits a barrier:

"Just don't tell me the wave is absorbed because I don't believe it."

"It fades away."

"Fades away, fades away, that's no excuse."

"What happens when your voice dies out?"

"Your voice dies out?"

"That's what I want to know."

"It dampens. It goes away."

"Where does it go?"

"It goes to voice heaven, right next to the wave heaven."

Some of the students in the class recognized that the energy from the wave must go somewhere, while others were content with the statement that it just disappeared. Eventually, the class voted in favor of two statements that they were willing to call "laws." The first, accepted almost unanimously, was "Waves pass through each other." The students had seen evidence of waves in springs and in water passing right through each other, so there was no question that it was true. The second statement, which commanded only a two-thirds vote, was "When a wave hits a barrier, part of it will bounce back, part of it will be absorbed by the barrier, and part of it may continue on." Although the statement made logical sense, fewer students were willing to support it because there was no direct evidence that it was always true.

After one of these discussion sessions it was not difficult to see what had to be done next. Often I'd present a mini-lecture to resolve conflicts, or offer an additional lab activity to test one of the students' ideas. Unless I was worried that the students would leave a class with more misconceptions than when they came, I refrained from pronouncing their statements to be true or false. I wanted the students to realize that scientific laws are not clear statements in the teacher's head or on the pages of a book but are hard-won discoveries gained from experimentation and logical argument (Sneider 1971).

The insight I learned that year was that it is extremely valuable for the teacher to sit on the sidelines as students discuss their interpretations of the phenomena. In these "minds-on" activities, the students seemed less inhibited in talking with each other than in answering the teacher's questions, and I could really focus on what they were saying, rather than planning what to say next. Later I developed more detailed content objectives, but I always tried to make time for these open-ended discussions about the phenomena that the students had been studying, taking myself out of the center of the discussion whenever possible. To summarize:

Insight #4 Structuring class discussions so students address each other rather than the teacher encourages students to express their own ideas and allows the teacher an opportunity to make observations and take notes on their thinking.

Culture Is Critical

In subsequent years I had the opportunity to attend graduate school at the University of California at Berkeley to earn a teaching credential and to learn about some of the excellent new curriculum materials that were just becoming available. Then, when I returned to teaching, I had the chance to integrate what I learned about examining student work with new curriculum materials in such diverse locations as San Jose, Costa Rica; the island of Pohnpei in Micronesia; and Coalinga, California.

An important insight that I gained from these experiences is that approaches developed within one cultural context do not necessarily translate to another. One of the clearest examples was my work in Micronesia, since the culture there was so different from life in the USA. The purpose of that program was to prepare high school students for colleges in the United States. But teaching classes in the American style was difficult since Micronesian teenagers are very shy. It was almost impossible to get a roaring class discussion going, even among college-bound seniors. I understood why this was so when I found that young people were actively discouraged from taking part in discussions at family gatherings. The right to speak in public was reserved for men over age 30. While hands-on activities were valuable in engaging the students' attention, it was difficult to understand the conversations among small groups of students when they preferred to speak their native language rather than English.

In my view, the most effective lessons were those in which the students created maps of their island, researched native crafts, and wrote stories and drew pictures about the rich history of their island. Especially compelling was a story about the origin of the island and its people, and the overall structure of the Pohnpean universe. Some of these were formatted as newsletters, translated from English into Pohnpean for the students to share with their parents and grandparents. Naturally it was not possible for us to check the students' Pohnpean translations, so we asked one of the parents for assistance. He made quite a few corrections and explained to us that in many cases the words used by young people to talk with each other were different from words used to address elders. Many of the corrections took into account who was talking to whom. By encouraging our students to undertake tasks that were meaningful for them, we learned enough about their culture to shift our methods and teaching objectives so as to create a bridge between the two cultures. The following statement sums up several teaching experiences that I've had where cultural differences have been an important factor.

Insight #5 The more we learn about our students' cultural backgrounds, the more successful we are likely to be in adjusting our teaching methods to meet their needs.

Study Group to Examine Student Work

The next chapter in my learning about how to really listen to students came when I returned to UC Berkeley for a graduate degree program. I happened to attend a seminar by Yossi Nussbaum, a visiting educator from Israel. He presented his research, conducted in collaboration with Jerome Novak from Cornell, that showed that children in the elementary–middle school range, in both Israel and New York, had very unusual notions about the spherical Earth concept. When asked about the shape of the Earth, nearly all children would say it is "round." However, on further probing, Dr. Nussbaum found a wide variety of different ideas. One child thought the Earth was round like an island. She explained that Columbus proved the Earth is round by sailing out of a port in Spain, going around the island, and back to the same port. Another realized that the Earth is round like a ball, but thought people lived just on top of the ball. When the sun went "under" the Earth, it sometimes caused volcanoes (Nussbaum and Novak 1976).

At the time I heard about Dr. Nussbaum's research I was teaching astronomy to a group of teachers. When I told them about these results they were incredulous. They explained to me that students learn the Earth is a sphere in the first or second grade, and they simply did not believe that any of their students would have difficulty with the concept. Three of the teachers agreed to work with me to conduct studies in their own classrooms. We formed a study group and conducted more than two hundred individual interviews and developed a paper-and-pencil questionnaire. Our study included children in grades four through nine. We examined the interview records and the written questionnaires very closely, both individually and as a group. Based on their responses to a series of open-ended questions, we classified the children's conceptions into several categories of ideas about the Earth's shape and gravity.

Sure enough, our results from the San Francisco Bay Area were consistent with Dr. Nussbaum's findings in New York and Israel. While there was deeper understanding of the spherical Earth concept among older students than younger students, there was a significant number of students at all age levels who failed to understand that we do indeed live on the outside surface of a ball and that objects fall "down" toward the center of the Earth (Sneider and Pulos 1983; Sneider et al. 1986).

The questionnaire had four questions. Question one asked why the Earth *looks* flat even though it is supposed to be round. Possible choices were taken from Nussbaum's paper and pilot studies. The second question asked children to imagine the Earth is made of glass so they could look right through it and to indicate what direction they would look to see people in far-off countries like China and India. The third question showed a drawing of Earth with enlarged humans standing all around it, each holding a rock. The students were asked to draw what would happen to the rock when each person dropped it and to explain their answers. The last question showed a hole drilled through the entire Earth, from pole to pole. The students were asked to draw the path of a rock dropped into the hole, and then to explain their answers.

While the results varied tremendously from class to class, a typical fifth-grade class had only five or six students who could answer all questions the way a scientist would. For Q1 these students would say that the "Earth is round like a ball but looks flat because we see only a small part of the ball." For Q2 they would show people looking downward, through the transparent Earth, to see people in far-off countries. For Q3 they would draw the rocks falling down to the surface of Earth and stopping at the people's feet. And for Q4 they would show the rock falling into the hole. Some would show the rock falling through the middle, then back again, finally settling in the middle. Others showed the rock simply falling to the middle and stopping. (Newton's laws of motion lead to the prediction that the rock will pass through the middle, then fall back and forth, settling in the middle. Most of the students who drew the rock falling to the center and stopping explained their answer by saying that's where the "center of gravity" is located.)

What was striking about the students whose answers did not agree with the scientists' was that they nonetheless reflected a consistent view of the world. For example, a student who indicated that Earth is like a flat, round island on the first question would indicate that a person would need to look parallel to the ground to see people in far-off countries. The student would then show rocks falling down, to the bottom of the page, in the next two questions. These answers are perfectly consistent with the conception of the Earth as a round island. Similarly, a student who indicated that the "Earth is round like a ball but looks flat because we see only a small part of the ball" might believe that people live just on top of the ball. That conception could be inferred by noting that they would look parallel to the ground to see people in far-off countries, and indicate rocks falling down to the bottom of the page in response to questions three and four.

At about that time I read a paper by Driver and Easley (1978) that recommended calling such ideas "alternative frameworks" rather than "misconceptions." Their perspective was that children's ideas were not wrong, even though their answers differed from those that would be given by scientists. When these students saw a globe in the classroom and were told by their teacher and textbook that the Earth is round, they created a personal theory of the world that integrated this new information with the flat Earth of their everyday experience. Some of their ideas that we uncovered through the interviews were marvelously inventive. Several of the children believed that the Earth is indeed shaped like a ball but that people live in the "flat part in the middle," with a hemispherical sky above and a hemispherical solid Earth below. That idea corresponded with illustrations in certain textbooks that illustrated how the path of the sun varied during the year. That same concept was reported by Dr. Nussbaum as a result of his interviews of children in Israel and New York.

Eventually, working with many teachers and colleagues at the Lawrence Hall of Science, we developed activities that enabled students to compare and contrast their ideas and to begin to recognize some of their own alternative frameworks. Using the questionnaire as a pre- and posttest revealed that most students from fourth through ninth grade who were involved in those activities gradually developed ideas that were more similar to scientists (Sneider and Ohadi 1998).

I gained two insights from those very detailed observations and long-term efforts to develop lessons that would change students' ideas about the Earth's shape and gravity. The first was that interviewing students and working closely with other teachers to examine the results of the interviews and written questionnaires is a tremendously rewarding activity. As individual teachers, we had never fully analyzed what our students were thinking. While it took quite a few evenings and weekends, we all agreed that forming a study group was worth the effort in terms of our own professional development and the insights it gave us into how our students think. In brief:

Insight #6 Study groups are an excellent way to compare interpretations of students' work.

Insight #7 Children are like scientists. They formulate theories to synthesize what they see and what they learn from others so that they have a consistent worldview. As teachers, our job is to help them articulate their current understanding and move to a more fruitful way of thinking.

Theories Are Not Easy to Change

The insight about how children construct theories of their world was reinforced in a very fortunate collaboration with two other astronomy educators, Varda Bar from Israel and Nathalie Martimbeau from Canada (Bar et al. 1994). During a casual conversation Dr. Bar mentioned a curious alternative conception about gravity that she found to be very common at the upper–elementary school level in Israel: that there is no gravity in space because there is no air up there (Bar et al. 1994). To support this belief many children refer to astronauts that they have seen on television who are floating around in space. Others refer to the smaller amount of gravity on the Moon, again assuming that is because there is no air on the Moon. Similar findings were reported by other investigators (Riggiero et al. 1985; Gunstone and White 1980; Watts 1982).

We designed a series of activities that could take place during a single class period that would help students articulate their current ideas about gravity, and experience logical conflicts that we hoped would lead them to abandon the idea that gravity requires air. We worked with two sixth-grade classes that had just finished a unit on astronomy. We interviewed a sample of ten students before and after presenting the unit, and we gave paper-and-pencil pre- and posttests to all of the students. Here is what two of the students said about gravity prior to the lesson about gravity:

Raymond (sixth grade, age 11)

Why does this pencil fall when you drop it?

"Gravity is pulling it down."

Why does a cloud not fall?

"It is very high in the atmosphere and it is not touching the gravity."

Why do the Moon and Sun not fall?

"The Moon is very high, past the Earth's atmosphere. The gravity stops at the top of the atmosphere. The same for the Sun."

What is gravity?

"It is the force that keeps us down. It is in the air."

Emily (sixth grade, age 11)

Why does this pencil fall when you drop it?

"Because of the gravity pulling it down."

Why does a cloud not fall?

"They are higher in the sky. They are made of condensation of water. They do not fall because gravity does not reach them."

Why do the Moon and Sun not fall?

"They are in space. There is no gravity there."

What is gravity?

"It is a pull, a thing that keeps … pushes things down on Earth or a planet. Air is around the Earth and keeps gravity. The atmosphere keeps the gravity inside."

We started class by having the students roll balls off tables, watching the curved path followed by the ball as it left the table. They saw that by pushing the ball faster and faster they could make it go further from the table before it hit the floor. The students were able to articulate that the path of the ball was due to its forward motion and the downward pull of gravity. We next showed a series of transparencies in which a baseball player hits a ball. The students explained that the ball would follow the same curved path as the balls that they rolled off of tables earlier in the class (though it might go further upward if it's a fly ball). The harder the ball is hit, the further it goes.

The baseball player in the transparency is then replaced by a cannon that is fired parallel to the Earth. As it is fired with greater and greater force, we asked the students what would happen to the cannon ball. Eventually the students saw that the cannon ball would circle the Earth completely, and go into orbit. We replaced the cannon ball with a space shuttle, and then the Moon, allowing the students to discuss these situations with each other, and providing coaching whenever we saw a good opportunity to do so. Near the end of the class we asked the students about gravity and air. If the space shuttle continues to circle the Earth as a result of gravity, then how could gravity depend on air? The same is true of the Moon. After the class, we gave the students a written questionnaire. We asked the students to write answers that indicated their personal beliefs, not just what other people said. The key question was: "Does gravity act in space where there is no air? Why or why not?" Here are the results of the students' answers.

Table 1. Responses to the Question "Does gravity act in space where there is no air? (Why or why not?)"

Does gravity act in space where there is no air?	Pretest	Posttest
Yes	13	23
No	31	10
Not Much	0	3
Only Near Planets	0	4
No Answer, or I Don't Know	4	8
Total	48	48

Note: The pretest was given at the beginning of the class period and the posttest was given one week after the class period. The subjects are 48 students in two groups of sixth graders.

Interviews with the same ten students whom we interviewed prior to the lesson confirmed the results of the questionnaire. On the posttest, there were more than twice as many "yes" answers as "no" answers. We have some confidence that students were giving us their honest opinions because most could give convincing reasons why gravity acts through space—for example, "Since the Earth keeps the Moon in orbit, there must be gravity in space." Another said, "This is why the planets go around the Sun."

Nonetheless, some students did not change their answers as a result of the lesson. They understood the first part of the activity, which concerned the rolling balls, but did not generalize it to include the notion of satellites around the Earth. However, even achieving this goal is a step in the right direction since, as we learn from the history of science, changing ideas about how things move here on Earth is the first step in learning about how things move in space.

An insight that we can draw from this experience is that it is very difficult for our students to change deep-seated ideas about the world that they have learned through a lifetime of experiences and that explain things in a way that is perfectly satisfactory to them. The students' ideas "work" for them, but they are quite different from what scientists have in mind when they speak of subjects such as orbits and weightlessness. For this reason we were not discouraged when we found that only some of our students were able to come to a more adequate understanding of how moons and space satellites stay in their orbits. For factual information or simpler concepts we might expect closer to 100 percent success; but for the development of fundamental concepts like gravity, we have to be more patient and expect that more such experiences, over a longer period of time, will be necessary to reach all of our students. To summarize:

Insight #8 Students are not likely to give up their deep-seated concepts of the world easily. Most will require a variety of learning experiences.

Insights and Outcomes

One of my most enriching experiences is the work that I have done for more than 15 years on a project at the Lawrence Hall of Science, UC Berkeley, entitled Great Explorations in Mathematics and Science (GEMS). In contrast to my science teaching experiences, in which I needed to have new lessons each day, working on the GEMS curriculum team gave me opportunities to repeat the same lessons several times with different groups of students and to observe the same science activities taught by different teachers. Several of us on the team compared notes, and together we would decide which changes should be made.

Among the many GEMS guides that I worked on, one of the most rewarding was about how to assess student learning. GEMS guides tend to focus on broad concepts, science and math thinking skills, and unifying ideas—and these are difficult to measure. The entire GEMS team collaborated on the development of a teacher's guide to the assessment of hands-on, minds-on activities. Our guide was entitled *Insights and Outcomes: Assessments for Great Explorations in Math and Science* (Barber et al.

1995). In the book we used 17 detailed cases studies to illustrate a variety of assessment methods, along with suggested rubrics for carefully examining and assigning values to students' work. From this work I learned the following:

> *Insight #9 There is a wide variety of ways to assess inquiry-based learning so as to measure progress against goals, and to inform next steps in instruction.*

Assessment or Instruction?

Now that I'm a museum administrator I tend to use the word "visitor" rather than "student" since we have a much greater diversity of learners than in a classroom. Learners for a given program or exhibit can range from five- or six-year-olds to teenagers, parents, and grandparents! While we attempt to design layers of meaning into our programs so there is something for everyone, we depend on a wide variety of techniques to examine our visitors' thinking. Here is one technique that works particularly well, even with a large group of museum visitors.

Ken Pauley, one of the museum's seasoned presenters of live programs, introduces a large snake and asks, "How much of this snake is tail, and how much is body?" To encourage visitors to respond, he explains that some people think it's all body; others say that it's all tail. During his presentation he allows time for just about everyone to respond to the question and leads them to discover knowledge that they already have to answer the question. ("Think of a dog or cat. What can we observe where the tail joins the body? Can we find similar structures on a snake? Would some volunteers care to come up and help me look for those structures?") Similarly, Jessica Swanson presents a mystery skull to the visitors and uses a series of questions to help them figure out what kind of animal it came from, based on such evidence as the positions of the eyes and kinds of teeth. The reader will probably recognize this teaching style as the Socratic questioning approach. Socrates may have been the first advocate in history for close examination of student work. What I love about the Socratic method is that it's impossible to distinguish between assessment and instruction. The answer to each question leads to the next question in a seamless flow of ideas. That reminds me of yet another insight:

> *Insight #10 Assessment can and should be an essential and inseparable aspect of instruction.*

Examining Cases

It seems appropriate to close with a recent project that is just coming to fruition. It is a video library created by WestEd, the Museum of Science, and WGBH-TV, with National Science Foundation support. The series of videos is entitled *Teachers as Learners: Professional Development in Science and Mathematics*. The purpose of the project is to provide vivid examples of a variety of strategies for designing professional development programs for teachers of science and mathematics. Working with the team that developed this video library greatly expanded my repertoire of professional development strategies. One of these was a case-study approach to closely examining student work. Used in this sense, a case study is an example of student work selected by a team of educators for the purpose of bringing to light key aspects of the teaching-learning process.

One tape in the series shows a group of about 20 teachers in a workshop organized by the Arizona Tribal Coalition. In the video we see a facilitator lead the group in applying a scoring rubric to the work of students for whom English is a second language. As various teachers suggest interpretations for what the students mean by their written answers, it becomes clear that they are learning a lot from each other. It is also clear that there is a great advantage if teachers understand the students' native language, so that errors in English are not interpreted as errors in scientific thinking. I gained two insights from that experience:

Insight #11 Examining prepared cases is a very powerful approach to acquiring skills in interpreting student work.

Insight #12 In the case of English language learners, it is helpful if we know the students' native language, so that errors in English are not interpreted as errors in scientific thinking.

Our Role as Teachers

The previous example is an appropriate way to end the chapter as it turns the spotlight from examining students' work to examining teachers' work. And the kind of teachers' work that is illuminated is the subject of this chapter—understanding what our students are thinking, so that we can help them develop more powerful ways of viewing the world. While it is clearly important for us to understand the concepts and skills we wish to teach, without a way of stepping inside our students' shoes it is impossible for us to communicate those concepts and skills in a deep and meaningful way.

References

Bar, V., B. Zinn, R. Goldmuntz, and C. Sneider. 1994. Children's concepts about weight and free fall. *Science Education* 78(3): 149–69.

Barber, J., L. Bergman, J. Goodman, K. Hosoume, L. Lipner, C. Sneider, and L.Tucker. 1995. *Insights and outcomes: Assessments for great explorations in math and science.* Berkeley: Lawrence Hall of Science, University of California at Berkeley.

Driver, R., and J. Easley. 1978. Pupils and paradigms: A review of literature related to concept development in adolescent science students. *Studies in Science Education* 5: 61–84.

Gunstone, R. F., and R. T. White. 1980. Understanding gravity. *Science Education* 65(3): 294–99.

Loucks-Horsley, S., P. Hewson, N. Love, and K. Stiles, with H. Dyasi, S. Friel, J. Mumme, C. Sneider, and K. Worth. 1998. *Designing professional development for teachers of science and mathematics.* Thousand Oaks, CA: Corwin Press.

National Research Council (NRC). 1996. *National science education standards*. Washington, DC: National Academy Press.

Nussbaum, Y., and J. Novak. 1976. An assessment of children's concepts of the Earth utilizing structured interviews. *Science Education* 60(4): 535–50.

Riggiero, S., A. Cartelli, F. Dupre, and M.Vincentini. 1985. Weight, gravity and air pressure: Mental representations by Italian middle school pupils. *European Journal of Science Education* 7(12): 181–94.

Sneider, C. 1971. A laboratory and discussion approach to high school science teaching. *The Physics Teacher* 9(1): 2–24.

———. 1972. A different discovery approach. *The Physics Teacher* 10(6): 327–29.

Sneider, C. I., and M. Ohadi. 1998. Unraveling students' misconceptions about the Earth's shape and gravity. *Science Education* 82: 265–84.

Sneider, C., and S. Pulos. 1983. Children's cosmologies: Understanding the Earth's shape and gravity. *Science Education* 67(2): 205–21.

Sneider, C., S. Pulos, E. Freenor, J. Porter, and B. Templeton. 1986. Understanding the Earth's shape and gravity. *Learning '86* 14(6): 43–47.

Teachers as learners: Professional development in science and mathematics. Video Library. In press. Thousand Oaks, CA: Corwin Press.

Watts, D. M. 1982. Gravity—Don't take it for granted! *Physics Education* 17(4): 116–21.

Additional Resources

The following books provide additional information, ideas, and activities for examining student work.

Atkin, J. M., P. Black, and J. Coffey, eds. 2001. *Classroom assessment and the national science education standards*. Washington, DC: National Academy Press.

Bar, V., C. Sneider, and N. Martimbeau. 1997. Is there gravity in space? *Science and Children* 34(7): 38–43.

Brown, J. H., and R. J. Shavelson. 1996. *Assessing hands-on science: A teacher's guide to performance assessment*. Thousand Oaks, CA: Corwin Press.

Doris, E. 1991. *Doing what scientists do: Children learn to investigate their world*. Portsmouth, NH: Heinemann.

Hein, G., and S. Price. 1994. *Active assessment for active science*. Portsmouth, NH: Heinemann.

Stead, K., and R. Osborne. 1981. What is gravity? Some children's ideas. *New Zealand Science Teacher* 30: 5–12.

Wolf, D., J. Bixby, J. Glenn III, and H. Gardner. 1992. To use their minds well: Investigating new forms of student assessment. *Review of Research in Education* 17: 31–74.

Assessment of Inquiry

Richard A. Duschl

Richard Duschl, professor of science education at King's College London, received his under-
graduate and doctorate degrees in Earth science education and science education, respectively,
from the University of Maryland–College Park. A former high school teacher, he served for 10
years as the editor of *Science Education*. His present research focuses on establishing science
assessment learning environments that focus on students' argumentation processes. This research
is an extension of the National Science Foundation–funded Project SEPIA (Science Education
through Portfolio Instruction and Assessment) research. Project SEPIA investigated the dynamic
structures of implementing full-inquiry units. Each unit is carefully written and researched to
involve students in solving a problem while developing and evaluating a scientific claim (e.g.,
causal explanation, model, argument). A focus of instruction is the epistemic criteria used to
evaluate knowledge claims.

> *"Of one thing I am convinced. I have never seen anybody improve in the art
> and techniques of inquiry by any means other than engaging in inquiry."*
> —Jerome Bruner, 1961

Teaching science through inquiry has been a distinguishing feature of innovative
science education programs since the 1960s science curriculum reform movement. Then, as now, however, the pedagogical challenges and material costs of teaching science as inquiry or science through inquiry minimized the number of classrooms
in which students learn science and learn about science through inquiry. Student-centered inquiry science teaching is complex and challenging. Assessing inquiry only
adds to the complexity and to the challenge. Part of the implementation problems teachers
face is deciding what type of instruction promotes inquiry teaching and what type of
instructional sequences and lessons count as inquiry curriculum.

Inquiry means many things to many different individuals. In fact, Table 2.6 in
Inquiry and the National Science Education Standards (NRC 2000) bears the title
"Essential Features of Classroom Inquiry and Their Variations." Some advocate the
use of inquiry methods to teach concepts while others propose their use to teach process skills. Still others associate inquiry learning with the completion of laboratory
investigations. But when we reflect on the five essential features of inquiry and on the
two National Science Education Standards K–12 inquiry goals (NRC 1996), namely,
"doing scientific inquiry" and "understanding scientific inquiry," the basic elements of
scientific inquiry become clearer. The focus on scientific inquiry needs to be on attainment of evidence and how it is used to generate and justify explanations.

Since the 1960s, research and scholarly findings in cognitive and social psychology (Bransford, Brown, and Cocking 2000; Pellegrino, Chudowsky, and Glaser 2001),
in history and philosophy of science (Magnani and Nersessian 1999), and in educational research (Linn and Hsi 2000; Millar, Leach, and Osborne 2001; Minstrell and
van Zee 2000) have developed new models of thinking and reasoning scientifically,
new models of science as a way of knowing, and new models of learning and teach-

ing science. When we synthesize this research, the messages we receive are the following:

1. The incorporation and assessment of scientific inquiry in educational contexts need to focus on three integrated domains:

   - the *conceptual* structures and cognitive processes used when reasoning scientifically,

   - the *epistemic* frameworks used when developing and evaluating scientific knowledge, and

   - the *social* processes and forums that shape how knowledge is communicated, represented, argued, and debated.

2. The conditions for science inquiry learning and assessment improve through the establishment of

   - learning environments that promote student-centered learning,

   - instructional sequences that promote integrating science learning across each of the three domains in item 1, above,

   - activities and tasks that make students' thinking visible in each of the three domains, and

   - teacher-designed assessment practices that monitor learning and provide feedback on thinking and learning in each of the three domains.

Research informs us that students come to our classrooms with a diversity of beliefs about the natural world and a diversity of skills for learning about the natural world. Research also tells us that accomplished teachers know how to take advantage of this diversity to enhance student learning and skill development. Accomplished teachers also know how to mediate student learning, that is, provide the helping hand and probing questions that enable students to move ahead in their understanding of conceptual structures, criteria for evaluating the status of knowledge claims, and strategies to communicate knowledge claims to others. Furthermore, accomplished teachers know how to create a classroom climate that promotes the sharing and display of students' ideas—thus making learners' thinking visible and teachers' assessment of inquiry possible.

The purpose of this chapter is to provide an overview of possible frameworks teachers can use to conduct assessments of students' engagement in scientific inquiry. In thinking about ways to conduct assessments around students' inquiry employing evidence to generate explanation, I will examine two factors. One is the design of classroom learning environments, by which is meant the curriculum, instruction, and assessment models that promote inquiry. The other factor is how to engage and facilitate students in thinking about the structure and communication of scientific information and knowledge (i.e., the conceptual, epistemic, and social domains). Herein, I maintain, lie the fundamentals of assessing scientific inquiry. The teacher needs to create a classroom learning environment that makes it possible to "listen to inquiry" and then employ a set of strategies that make it possible to give feedback on students' use of scientific information and the construction and evaluation of scientific knowledge claims. Adapting the opening quote by Bruner, I can think of no other way for teachers to learn how to assess inquiry other than engaging in the task of assessing inquiry.

Listening to Inquiry

Teaching in a manner that promotes scientific inquiry is much more than providing and managing materials and activities for students to conduct investigations. Engaging students in kit-based science or lab investigations in and of itself is not inquiry. More often than not, kit-based and lab science lessons are designed to confirm through a final-form science approach what it is we already know. The kind of inquiry I want us to consider is that which occurs when students examine how scientists have come to know what they believe to be scientific knowledge and why they believe this knowledge over other competing knowledge claims. Such instruction is grounded in a consideration of what counts as evidence and as explanations.

Scientific inquiry that goes beyond teaching the facts or what we know provides opportunities for students to share, discuss, debate, and argue the complex set of ideas, information, beliefs, and questions they bring to or learn in the classroom. Designing, establishing, and managing assessment-driven science inquiry learning environments, however, is difficult (Krajcik et al. 1994; Duschl and Gitomer 1997; Black and Wiliam 1998). Consider the following excerpt from the *National Science Education Standards:*

> *Students at all grade levels and in every domain of science should have the opportunity to use scientific inquiry and develop the ability to think and act in ways associated with inquiry, including asking questions, planning and conducting investigations, using appropriate tools and techniques to gather data, thinking critically and logically about relations between evidence and explanations, constructing and analyzing alternative explanations, and communicating scientific arguments.* (NRC 1996, 105)

A prerequisite for assessing students' inquiry is creating a learning environment that gives inquiry a voice. Assessing inquiry requires creating conditions that allow teachers, and eventually the students themselves, to listen to inquiry. The string of inquiry abilities in the above excerpt gives us some guidance about what we need to accomplish in the design of our classroom learning environments. The key ideas in the quote are from the "Changing Emphases to Promote Inquiry" table found in the *National Science Education Standards*, presented here as Figure 1.

Figure 1. Changing Emphases to Promote Inquiry

More Emphasis on

- Activities that investigate and analyze science questions
- Investigations over extended periods of time
- Process skills in context
- Using multiple process skills—manipulation, cognitive, procedural
- Using evidence and strategies for developing or revising an explanation
- Science as argument and explanation
- Communicating science explanations
- Groups of students often analyzing and synthesizing data after defending conclusions
- Doing more investigations in order to develop understanding, ability, values of inquiry and knowledge of science content
- Applying the results of experiments to scientific arguments and explanations
- Management of ideas and information
- Public communication of student ideas and work to classmates

---

Source: National Research Council (NRC). 1996. *National science education standards.* Washington, DC: National Academy Press, p. 113.

The assessment of inquiry is best thought of as a set of elements that place emphasis on examining the *processes* of engaging in scientific knowing and learning, as opposed to the *products* or outcomes of scientific knowing and learning. Scientific inquiry is fundamentally ill-structured. We may have an initial question and some sense of the data we need, but with time and experience the inquiry is shaped and modified. Inquiry is foremost a journey that begins with a set of guiding conceptions and questions that lead us through the attainment and examination of data. When we look at the list of "more emphasis on" items in Figure 1, we get a sense of what needs to happen to make listening to inquiry possible. Investigations are long term and process skills are not limited to the traditional Science—A Process Approach (SAPA) skills for conducting investigations (e.g., observing, using numbers, generating hypotheses, making and reading graphs, etc.) but also include consideration of the cognitive skills and epistemic criteria that frame scientific reasoning and decision-making. For an excellent review of research on young children's inquiry abilities, see Metz (1998), who writes,

> *Children at the first level of schooling are capable of independent empirical investigations that, while falling short of older children and adults in adequacy of experimental design and inference, support both fruitful theory construction and the improvement of the inquiry process itself. Even before instruction, many aspects of children's theorising resemble the theorising of scientists.* (85)

The crux of the matter is simple to state but complex to implement and manage. Teachers need to develop new ways of listening to and monitoring students' scientific reasoning and thinking. A key component in the design of inquiry learning environments is developing or using extended (two- to four-week-long) instructional contexts. Table 1 presents information on a set of science inquiry units developed with support from the National Science Foundation. Most are web-based, thus providing easy access for review. What you will find in all of these inquiry units is a compelling inquiry context or problem to facilitate students' meaningful engagement in inquiry lessons. Another important design feature of the units in Table 1 is the incorporation of formative assessment tasks and activities into the instructional sequence that help make visible students' thinking. Here the challenge is developing students' abilities for communicating and representing what they know and how and why they believe what they know. White and Gunstone's *Probing Understanding* (1992) is a useful resource here for teachers. Each of the main chapters outlines how a different instruction strategy (e.g., concept maps, drawings, interviews, demonstrating) can be used to probe and monitor students' understanding. Many examples of student work are provided. As students become more adept at communicating and representing scientific information, teachers will, in turn, be in a better position to listen and give feedback. It is a symbiotic relationship.

Yet another important learning environment component to support inquiry is that of teachers, and eventually students themselves, developing and employing analytical insights and criteria for assessing the thinking and the scientific inquiry being revealed. Here is where my adaptation of Bruner's quote applies. Teachers need to begin listening to inquiry and then develop and apply criteria that engage learners in deciding "what counts" as evidence and as explanations.

In summary, an important aspect of assessing inquiry is designing the learning environment to promote inquiry activities and students' reporting and sharing information and ideas. In the next sections of the chapter we will examine two strategies for targeting assessment of inquiry. First, we consider in more detail how science inquiry is a process of transition from evidence to explanation. Then we consider strategies for supporting assessment conversations with students. Here we consider the importance of conducting assessments in the three domains—conceptual, epistemic, and social—that frame scientific inquiry.

Evidence and Explanation

Science distinguishes itself from other ways of knowing by appealing to evidence that is deemed objective by its practitioners and then using the evidence to put forth testable explanations. Scientific ideas and information are rooted in evidence and guided by our best-reasoned beliefs in the form of the scientific theories that frame investigations and inquiries. All elements of science—questions, methods, evidence, and explanations—are open to scrutiny, examination, justification, and verification. *Inquiry and the National Science Education Standards* (NRC 2000) identifies five essential features of classroom inquiry, which are presented in Figure 2.

Table 1. National Science Foundation–Supported Full-Inquiry Science Units

Curriculum Project and Web Address	Project Leader	Description of Units
LeTUS—Learning Technologies in Urban Schools *www.letus.org*	Louis Gomez, Brian Reiser, and Daniel Edelson, Northwestern U.	Middle- and secondary-level inquiry-based units on climate, air quality, solar energy, Create-a-World.
Learning by Design *www.cc.gatech.edu/projects/lbd/*	Janet Kolodner, Georgia Tech U.	Middle school; physical and Earth science units designed around case-based reasoning.
WISE—Web-based Inquiry Science Environment *wise.berkeley.edu*	Marcia Linn and Jim Slotta U. of California, Berkeley	Grades 5–12; 2-week capstone units; 13 projects in physical, life, and Earth science.
One Sky, Many Voices *www.onesky.umich.edu*	Nancy Songer, U. of Michigan	K–12; environmental focus; 4–8-week units; Kids as Global Scientists, BioKids.
MUSE—Modeling for Understanding in Science Education *www.wcer.wisc.edu*	Jim Stewart, U. of Wisconsin	Secondary biology and Earth science; extended 9-week courses; units on genetics, evolution.
SEPIA—Science Education through Portfolio Instruction and Assessment e-mail: *richard.duschl@kcl.ac.uk*	Richard Duschl, King's College London	Middle school; 4–6-week problem-based inquiry units; units on flotation, acid/base chemistry, earthquakes, and volcanoes.
BioLogica *biologica.concord.org*	Concord Consortium	High school; independent inquiry and scientific reasoning; units on genetics, cell, DNA.
Hi-CE—Center for Highly Interactive Computing in Education *hi-ce.eecs.umich.edu*	Joseph Krajcik, U. of Michigan	Middle and high school; modeling software (e.g., Science Laboratory) to investigate complex problems.
BGuILE—Biology GUided Inquiry Learning Environments *www.letus.org/bguile/*	Brian Reiser, Northwestern U.	Middle and high school; scientific investigation and argumentation using puzzling and authentic problems; units on evolution, animal behavior.

Figure 2. Essential Features of Classroom Inquiry

- Learners are engaged by scientifically oriented questions.
- Learners give priority to **evidence**, which allows them to develop and evaluate explanations that address scientifically oriented questions.
- Learners formulate **explanations** from evidence to address scientifically oriented questions.
- Learners evaluate their explanations in light of alternative explanations, particularly those reflecting scientific understanding.
- Learners communicate and justify their proposed explanations.

Source: National Research Council (NRC). 1996. *National science education standards.* Washington, DC: National Academy Press, p. 25.

The emphasis in Figure 2 on the words *evidence* and *explanations* appears in the original. Science at its core is fundamentally about acquiring data and then transforming that data first into evidence and then into explanations. The point I want to make here is that preparation for making scientific discoveries and engaging in scientific inquiry is linked to students' opportunities to examine the development and unfolding or transformations of data across the evidence-explanation (EE) continuum. The EE continuum and three transformations are presented in Figure 3. The strategy I propose is to allow students to make and report judgments, reasons, and decisions

---

Figure 3. Scientific Inquiry and Communication Processes

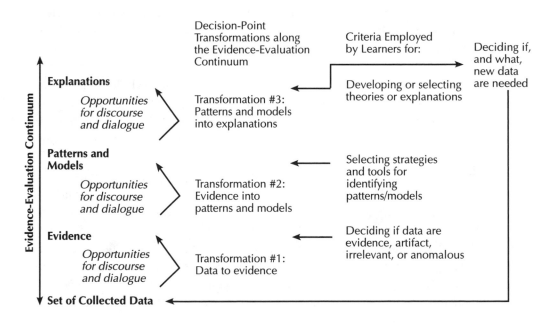

during three critical transformations in the EE continuum. One is selecting data to become evidence. Two is analyzing evidence to generate models and/or locate patterns of evidence. Three is locating or otherwise determining the scientific explanations that account for the models and patterns of evidence.

At each of the three transformations, students are encouraged to share their thinking by engaging in argument, representation and communication, and modeling and theorizing. At each transformation, teachers are to engage in assessments of inquiry by comparing and contrasting student responses to each other and, importantly, to the instructional aims, knowledge structures, and goals of the science unit. In other words, effective assessments of science inquiry examine students' beliefs and decision-making concerning the transformations of data to evidence, evidence to patterns or models, and patterns/models to explanation.

Another reason to adopt the EE continuum as an instructional framework for guiding the planning and/or design of curriculum, instruction, and assessment models is that it helps slow down the pace of instruction and, thus, helps facilitate assessment of inquiry. The unfolding of data takes time and this is another reason why effective inquiry units are longer in length. When teachers pause to allow students to come together and discuss and debate what they know, what they believe, and what evidence they have to support their ideas, thinking is made visible, thus enabling monitoring and assessments of the communication of information and of the thinking.

The commitment here is to curriculum frameworks that (1) promote full or extended instructional sequences rather than partial or short, single-lesson instructional sequences and (2) intentionally embed into the instructional sequence assessment-driven activities that facilitate feedback on the conceptual, epistemic, and social goals of the unit. Again, the units presented in Table 1 are good examples of curriculum material that do this. Typically, we are looking at units that are two to four weeks in length, sometimes longer. The additional time is needed to make room for student conversations and representations of reasoning that, in turn, make possible assessments of inquiry. The significant trade-off that needs to be made is holding down the number of concepts, science terms, and labels so that the data-driven elements of scientific inquiry can be examined and debated. The National Science Education Standards recommend that at each grade level K–12 students be given the opportunity to complete at least one full-inquiry unit.

When core scientific concepts are kept to a minimum (e.g., in the curriculum designs for Project SEPIA [Science Education through Portfolio Instruction and Assessment] [Duschl and Gitomer 1997] a maximum of 20 core concepts frame the inquiry), students' thinking can shift from memorization of terms to the important tasks of knowledge integration and the development of criteria for evaluating scientific knowledge claims. Let's consider in more detail how the three transformations promote assessment opportunities. During full-inquiry instructional sequences we want students to probe how raw data from investigations are analyzed and selected to be evidence, how evidence is selected and analyzed to identify patterns, trends, and models, and how patterns, trends, and models are selected and analyzed to generate scientific explanations. Each is an important "transitional" step or transformation in doing science. Each transition involves asking students to commit to judgments about "what counts" and thus makes visible students' thinking and beliefs about "what counts." Assessments of inquiry on each of the three domains—conceptual, epistemic, and social—can now take place.

Fundamentally important to the success of conducting assessments along the EE continuum is capturing the diversity of thinking found in students' judgments and decisions. One important dynamic is to always ask students to provide reasons and evidence to back up the judgments and decisions they make. When students are asked to explain or justify their results, judgments, and decisions with reasons and evidence, their thinking is made visible and several important assessments of inquiry can occur. For example, a common strategy for making students' thinking visible is to ask each student or group of students, upon completion of an investigation, to place their data into a class data table on a board or overhead transparency or in a computer data file. Making public the display of data facilitates discussion about what data to use as evidence. The class data table may reveal, among other things, errors and successes in measurement and in data recording (e.g., placement of decimal points, use of formulas). Students can begin to sense patterns in the data (e.g., the second transformation in the EE continuum). Discussion about the class data table may reveal that more data are needed to complete the inquiry or that the data being collected can't be used to answer the questions being posed.

Through the discussion of data, mediated and guided by the teacher, students begin to develop a sense of the criteria for good data. Students begin to learn that scientific inquiry involves asking questions of the data and using the data to ask new questions. Full-inquiry instructional sequences make provisions for just such occurrences. An excellent source of instructional strategies to use with students for handling the analysis and reporting of data is *Investigating Real Data in the Classroom* (Lehrer and Schauble 2002).

Another instructional strategy that promotes assessments of what counts as data and evidence is providing students with options for obtaining data and then asking them to justify their choices. The choices and the reasons provided to support choices create another kind of assessment opportunity about students' thinking and reasoning. Many kit-based science investigations, in the interest of allowing time to "cover" the content, are structured so that all students use the same equipment, probe the same question, and use the same materials. When the outcomes are the same, what is there to discuss and debate? Monolithic knowledge does not engender scientific reasoning or critical thinking. The goal during science inquiry lessons is to create conditions that stimulate diversity among students' responses. A key dynamic to effective assessment of inquiry is exposing the different reasons and beliefs that students hold in order to encourage communication of ideas and argumentation about ideas, both essential features of scientific inquiry.

Consider the example of the "Acids and Bases" middle school unit (Erduran 1999) designed as part of Project SEPIA. To promote diversity of outcomes and thus create assessment conversation opportunities, we decided to provide students with six different techniques for determining acidity and alkalinity early in the unit. Making students' thinking visible at this point in the instructional sequence allowed for an assessment of students' comprehension of the unit goals and their thinking about "what counts" as good data.

The performance goals for the six-week, full-inquiry "Acids and Bases" unit were to identify five unknown substances as either acids or bases and then devise a strategy for safe disposal. A core concept was neutralization since safe disposal depends on neutralization. The six techniques were used to test known substances, and students were told that the goal of the lesson was to decide which technique(s) would be best to use with the unknown samples. Only two of the six techniques for testing the unknowns could determine if a solution was neutral. After testing all six techniques, students were asked to select, and give reasons for choosing, the technique they believed to be best.

The students' lab reports and the oral discussions that followed were quite revealing. First, each of the techniques was considered "best" by at least some of the students, and thus we achieved the requisite diversity of thinking to hold an assessment conversation. For some, litmus paper was the choice because it was fast and easy. Bromothymol blue and yellow were the choice of others because these were judged to be pretty and fascinating. These were interesting perspectives but not grounded in scientific reasoning nor attentive to the inquiry goals of the unit's problem. The second way the students' reports were revealing is they made visible students' thinking, that is, that some students had lost sight of the goal of the full-inquiry. Given the research that shows teachers' goals for lessons and students' perceptions of the goals of lessons are frequently not the same (Osborne and Freyberg 1985), we felt the diversity of student responses provided a timely chance to conduct an assessment conversation that focused on long-term conceptual and epistemic goals of the inquiry unit.

Neutralization is the important guiding concept for this problem-based inquiry unit, but only about 25 percent of the students demonstrated such awareness or understanding. The teacher and I sat down and sorted the lab reports into piles based on students' reasons for choice of method. Examining students' work and deciding how it will be used to promote learning are the first steps in carrying out an assessment of inquiry. By surveying and selecting samples of student work that reflected the diversity of thinking, we were able to plan a whole class discussion on the best methods for gathering data. The second step in carrying out an assessment of inquiry is to make the diversity of students' thinking visible to the class. Asking students themselves to examine the range of responses—followed by a teacher-led class discussion—made students' thinking visible. Through the oral testimonies of students and via debates over alternative perspectives, students who were off-track on the unit goals were brought back on track. Additionally, the assessments of students' thinking by the students themselves help them see how the goals of the inquiry (e.g., understanding neutralization for safe disposal) help determine "what counts" as good data. Subtle, yes, but an important step in aiding students to make progress on the standard "Developing students' understandings about scientific inquiry" (NRC 1996).

The third way students' reports from the six-techniques activity were revealing had to do with the introduction of new concepts by the students into the classroom learning environment. When given the chance to communicate what they know and believe, students will surprise you in what they bring to a discussion. Furthermore, the fact that concepts come from students, rather than the textbook or the teacher, means that the inquiry begins to rest with the students and important connections are made. This is a powerful dynamic in shaping a science inquiry learning environment because students begin to own the ideas. In this lesson, students who selected pH paper or Universal Indicator did so because, in the words of one student, "It tells you how much of an acid it is" and of another, "You know how much acid or base is in it." To the astute teacher who knows acid and base chemistry, such comments are steppingstones to developing an understanding of the pH scale and the concept of ions (H^+, OH^-).

Instructional sequences can be designed to promote assessments of scientific inquiry by having students report on their ideas, beliefs, and reasons. A key element of science inquiry units that promote formative assessments is designing activities and tasks that promote teacher "listening" and do so over time in each of the three assessment domains—conceptual, epistemic, and social. Fill-in-the-blank worksheets and responses to multiple-choice questions may help with feedback on simple concept learning but do little to promote feedback on the conceptual, epistemic, or social domains associated with scientific inquiries that seek links between evidence and explanation.

Assessment Conversations in Three-Part Harmony

Up to this point, the emphasis has been on designing learning environment conditions that help teachers to carry out assessments of inquiry. Let's now turn our attention to some practical issues—namely, the domains of assessments a teacher needs to consider and a strategy teachers can use to facilitate assessment conversations on scientific inquiry. The chapter opened with references to three important domains to consider when setting out to establish a classroom learning environment that will promote the assessment of inquiry.

- *Conceptual Domain.* First, there is the need to have access to information that will allow you to assess both (a) the conceptual frameworks you want students to learn and use and (b) the alternative conceptual frameworks students naturally bring with them to lessons. Students, like scientists, come to any inquiry with a set of beliefs and commitments that guide them in reasoning and decision-making. Effective science teachers will continually assess pupils' conceptual understandings. Scientific inquiry typically requires knowledge integration across several areas of science and ways of reasoning. The design of curriculum activities and tasks should promote teachers' access to students' reasoning about science concepts and to students' use of science concepts.

- *Epistemic Domain.* Second, there is the need to have access to information that will allow you to assess the epistemic frameworks students use during an inquiry. Epistemic frameworks are the knowledge structures (e.g., data, evidence, principles, theory) and the rules and criteria used in scientific inquiry for determining "what counts" as a good experiment, measurement, graph, explanation, or argument, to name but a few products of inquiry. When we ask students to develop and evaluate experiments, evidence, hypotheses, explanations, models, or arguments, we are asking them to employ epistemic frameworks.

- *Social Domain.* Third, there is the need to have access to information that will allow the teacher to assess the representation and communication frameworks students will need to use while engaging in inquiry. Here the goal is to make thinking visible through oral, written, and pictorial presentations of concepts, conceptual frameworks, and criteria that frame the inquiry. The more accomplished students get at communicating and showing what they know, then the more accomplished teachers can get at listening to students' thinking and providing assessments of inquiry. Deliberation and discourse need to be a central part of the classroom learning environment.

Let's turn once again to the Essential Features of Classroom Inquiry as presented in Figure 2 and consider how each inquiry feature is related to the three assessment domains. The conceptual frameworks students use will influence each of the five features, but, in particular, students' conceptual frameworks will affect Feature 1. The research on alternative conceptions tells us how important it is to work with students' ideas. Construction of concept maps is one instructional strategy for making thinking visible and assessing how learners are integrating knowledge. Other useful strategies for promoting assessment of the conceptual frameworks students bring to science lessons are activities that engage them in design activities or problem-solving while employing scientific ideas and information. When students are given assignments that ask them to provide reasons or evidence to support design or problem-solving decisions, conceptual commitments are exposed and feedback is possible.

Yet another way to make visible students' thinking about conceptual frameworks is through question generation. After establishing the initial "focus question" for a scientific inquiry, making room in lessons to allow students to ask new questions and hear others asking subsequent questions sheds light on students' reasoning. But each of these strategies has to be modeled by the teacher and nurtured through assessment practices. Students do not arrive knowing how to do concept maps or how to ask questions. Teachers need to help them learn how to communicate and represent ideas with concept maps. Here is an instance where there is overlap with the conceptual and social domain.

The epistemic frameworks address Features 2, 3, and 4. With a focus on three of the five essential features, epistemic frameworks are clearly important. Again, providing opportunities for students to give reasons is a strategy that makes thinking visible. The epistemic frameworks teachers need to develop among students are such things as the notion of a fair test or why we use models to tell us things about the real world (Schauble et al. 1995). Epistemic frameworks function at each of the three data transformations. Decisions about evidence, patterns in evidence, and explanations of evidence are all influenced by choices that determine "what counts" as good/sound evidence, patterns, and explanations. We know, for example, that when confronted with a set of data or evidence, many students will seek information that confirms a personal view and ignore the information that refutes their point of view (Metz 1998). Assessment practices can help make such faulty thinking visible to learners.

Epistemic frameworks also include the development of the criteria students are to use to make judgments about ideas and information. A simple criterion is to ask students if they can give an example or cite an instance when they have seen an idea or a phenomenon before. A more sophisticated criterion is to ask students to statistically determine if a reported finding is typical or if it is an outlier for the data being generated.

Clearly, the representation and communication frameworks are related to Feature 5. A critically important challenge for teachers seeking to develop their abilities to assess scientific inquiry is to learn the ways to display and represent data and information. Visualization techniques for the presentation and representation of data and information help promote thinking and making thinking visible. There is growing interest in the use of exploratory data analysis (EDA) techniques with K–12 science students. Initially developed for statisticians, EDA techniques such as stem-and-leaf and box-and-whisker diagrams are proving successful with helping students see the shape of data and the typical patterns in data. Again, Lehrer and Schauble's book (2002) is an excellent source of examples of elementary-level students using various EDA techniques to discuss data. In turn, these displays of data help promote assessments that can, for example, help students learn about mathematical modeling and statistical probabilistic reasoning.

The best teachers are those who can assess where a learner is in his or her knowledge development and then provide the right intervention to advance the learner. Assessing and advancing learning is mediation of learning. The general consensus among educational researchers (Bransford, Brown, and Cocking 2000; Pellegrino, Chudowsky, and Glaser 2001) is that the most effective learning environments are those that support mediation of learning. In school science, the enterprise of addressing epistemic connections and other elements of inquiry is about carefully designed learning sequences that engage students in doing science (e.g., investigations, problems, and projects). But doing science is also about engaging students in colloquiums or conversations around the investigations, problems, and projects. As we have already discussed, there are important inquiry steps between obtaining the raw data of observation and acquiring the theory-informed selection of evidence used to develop explanations, theories, and models. Richard Grandy (1997), in a critique of the popular constructivist practices in science classroom, warns that

> *[w]hat is missing [from most constructivist teaching models] are the epistemic connections that relate theory to supporting data, to conflicting theories, to anomalous data, to equivocal data.... What can be taken as data and what is disqualified, what is strong evidence and what is weak evidence, is always judged against the background provided by the community's experience with the theories, the data domain, and the instruments in question.... The demarcation between what counts and what does not ... is critical to the ongoing enterprise.* (49–50)

Grandy is reinforcing the ideas presented above that stress the notion that good science teaching requires a focus on the refinement and extension of ideas about "what counts." Up to this point the discussion has been on evidence and explanation. Now we turn our attention to the language of the classroom. We are talking about developing among students the discriminating language that promotes doing scientific inquiry and understanding scientific inquiry. It is a language, for example, where students are comfortable speaking about the shape, spread, range, mean, mode, median, and outliers of data sets. It is a language that builds arguments supported by premises that, in turn, are supported by backings and evidence.

The call for conversations is a recognition of the value and importance that representation, communication, and evaluation play in science learning. I use *conversation* in a very broad sense to include, among others ideas, argumentation, debate, modeling, drawing, writing, and other genres of language. Such an expanded repertoire helps us to consider an important domain of research in both formal and informal science learning settings, namely, how to mediate the learning experiences. The position advanced by Schauble, Leinhardt, and Martin (1997), and adopted here, is that such learning mediations should focus on promoting talk, activity structures, signs and symbol systems, or, collectively, what I wish to call conversations. For science learning, the conversations should mediate the transitions from evidence to explanations, do so within the salient conceptual domain, and, thereby, unfold discovery and inquiry.

The idea of conversations or colloquiums in science classrooms is taken from Lansdown, Blackwood, and Brandwein (1971). Grounded in Vygotsky's theory of learning that claims meaning is obtained through language, colloquiums are "speaking together" opportunities that begin with "a pooling of observations, getting a collection of facts into the arena, so to speak, to make individuals aware of common data seen from different viewpoints. This is the beginning of speaking together." (Lansdown,

Blackwood, and Brandwein 1971, 120). Speaking together activities can be whole class events, small group activities, or interactive, computer-supported learning contexts. In each instance, the conversations present "listening to inquiry" opportunities. Speaking together opportunities, when properly planned and managed, are also wonderful occasions for making thinking visible. You will find that the curriculum units listed in Table 1 (p. 45) have designed formats for supporting science conversations.

In Project SEPIA, the speaking together occasions take place during instructional episodes we call assessment conversation activities. The assessment conversation is an idealized model of teaching practice. These conversations are structured discussions in which student products and reasoning are made public, recognized, and used to develop questions and activities that can (a) promote conceptual growth for students and (b) provide assessment information to the teachers. The assessment conversation has three general stages, presented in Table 2. The first stage is to *receive* student ideas. This requires that students be allowed to represent their understanding as fully as possible. To this end, SEPIA instruction incorporates detailed writing, drawing of annotated pictures, linkages between drawings and writings, construction of storyboards, and many other techniques that allow students to show what they know.

Table 2. Stages of the Assessment Conversation

Stage	Description
Stage 1: Receiving Information	• Individual or group efforts on specialized tasks that by design bring about a diversity of student responses and range of representation or ideas. • Teacher and students make explicit and publicly display via posters, presentations, charts, overheads, and so forth the diversity of students' efforts, representations of meanings and understandings, and performances on the tasks.
Stage 2: Recognizing Information	• Teacher examines critically and makes an appraisal of the diversity of student efforts, meanings, understanding, and performances and selects student work according to goal domains (conceptual, epistemic, social) to be addressed. • Teacher and students work toward a synthesis of what counts or stands for appropriate efforts, meanings, understandings, and performances employing agreed upon criteria.
Stage 3: Using Information	• Applying what has been learned to an evaluation of previous efforts, meanings, understandings, and performances or to the design of a new investigation for advancing efforts, meanings, understandings, and performances in the present domain of inquiry.

Once the students have represented their understanding, it is the responsibility of the teacher to *recognize* the ideas (Stage 2) in the classroom in relation to unit or lesson goals. Inevitably, there will be a diversity of ideas. In traditional classrooms, this diversity is quickly constrained through an appeal to find the "best answer." In a full-inquiry unit that supports assessment conversations, diversity is made public and resolved through a discussion that is governed by scientific criteria and evidence. In this second step of an assessment conversation, the students' ideas and information are publicly shared (e.g., displayed on overhead, copied and distributed to student groups) and discussed. Here the teacher needs to intervene to select the samples of student work to bring to the attention of students. The teacher also needs to decide the focus of the assessment conversation depending on the inquiry goals (e.g., conceptual, epistemic, social) that she or he wishes to pursue at this time.

In recognizing the diversity of student work, teachers need to select work that differs on dimensions relevant to the conceptual, epistemic, and social domain(s) being explored. The teacher must guide the class through a discussion in which the critical differences in student representations and reasoning are highlighted. Consider, for example, the storyboards in Figure 4. The three storyboards are from a seventh-grade class that was studying flotation and buoyancy using the "Vessels" SEPIA unit. Students were directed to draw (storyboard), in as many frames as they wished, the action of and forces acting on a ball released under water. As you can see, each is quite different and revealing. The two principal goals for the "Vessels" SEPIA unit are (1) designing a vessel hull that maximizes carrying capacity and (2) developing a causal explanation for why vessels can float while carrying a load.

With regard to the conceptual goals of the unit, we can examine Storyboard #3 and discuss the omission of gravity forces whenever the ball is under the water. Is this accurate? The other two storyboards show gravity acting on the ball when it is under the water. Which depiction is correct? We can also ask what role water displacement has in the physics of flotation and buoyancy. With regard to the social goals of the unit, we can compare Storyboard #1 with #2 and #3. Storyboards #2 and #3, respectively, use length of arrow and number of arrows to describe the forces acting on the ball. Further, Storyboard #3 uses a key (G = gravity). Students can discuss how the use of arrows, labels, symbols, and narration helps to communicate scientific ideas.

When we ask students about the information in their drawings, thinking is made visible and mediated learning occurs. Middle school students, however, are quite reluctant to discuss each other's work in public. Through our research, we have found it useful for teachers to import student work from other classrooms for purposes of assessment conversations. When the author is anonymous, students are good to go.

Once the diversity of ideas is public, the teacher can *use* that diversity (Stage 3) as a basis for achieving a consensus view in the classroom. The teacher poses questions and facilitates a discussion that results in the consensus. Generally, one group of students' representation or reasoning is viewed as satisfying operating criteria more than other students' (e.g., it is more consistent with the evidence). A final use

Figure 4. Storyboards: Students Draw the Action of and Forces Acting on a Ball under Water

Storyboard #1

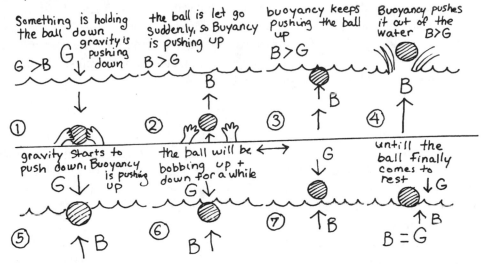

Storyboard #2

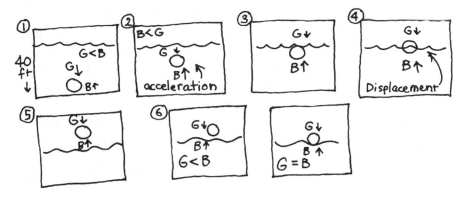

Storyboard #3

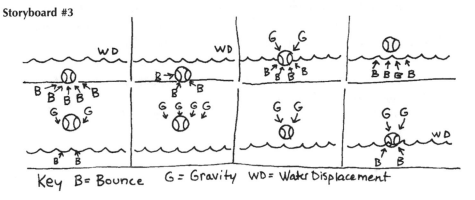

of student understanding is to entertain how the accepted view may generalize to new and different situations. In Storyboards #1 and #2 the arrows are drawn straight up and down while in Storyboard #3 the forces are depicted acting as a cluster around the submerged object in one upward direction but buoyant pressure acts on a submerged object in all directions. This is a subtle but important distinction for developing a causal explanation for why a vessel can float carrying a load. Storyboard #3 can be used to advance students' thinking about the role water pressure has on flotation and buoyancy (e.g., the greater the depth, the greater the water pressure) and on the design of a vessel that incorporates high sides.

Summary

The assessment of inquiry is a complex task. We have discussed the importance of organizing classroom learning environments and using instructional sequences that support "listening to inquiry." We have examined some characteristics of instructional sequences that promote inquiry. We have discussed how teachers need to support assessments across three domains—conceptual, epistemic, and social—to make thinking about doing science visible.

Successful assessment-driven learning environments create a symbiotic relationship between teacher and students. As the teacher mediates learning, students' knowledge and skills for communicating develop. This, in turn, enables the teacher to mediate learning at new, more complex levels of inquiry. In time, the students will learn from each other as well. Effective mediation on the part of the teacher, though, in addition to everything that has been discussed, also demands a strong understanding of the subject matter and of the inquiry goals for the instructional sequence.

One key to success with assessing inquiry is to give students a voice and then teach them how to use that voice. Another key to success is for teachers to learn how to listen to and make sense of student voices. In our science and technology world, our students know much more than we give them credit for. Deficit, "my students can't do that" models of learners must be replaced by more open and supportive images. When you allow the conversation of science to open up along the evidence-to-explanation continuum and examine the three transformations, you will be amazed at the depth and breadth of ideas and information your students will bring to the debate. Thus, the assessment of inquiry must be situated in carefully designed instructional sequences that support conversations about evidence and explanations and that offer ongoing assessment opportunities. So, take a look at the instructional units in Table 1 and get in the game. The only way to get better at the art of assessing inquiry is to begin assessing inquiry.

References

Black, P., and D. Wiliam. 1998. Assessment and classroom learning. *Assessment in Education* 5(1): 7–73.

Bransford, J., A. Brown, and R. Cocking, eds. 2000. *How people learn: Brain, mind, experience, and school.* Washington, DC: National Academy Press (*http://www.nap.edu*).

Bruner, J. 1961. The act of discovery. *Harvard Educational Review* 31: 21–32.

Duschl, R., and D. Gitomer. 1997. Strategies and challenges to changing the focus of assessment and instruction in science classrooms. *Educational Assesssment* 4(1): 37–73.

Erduran, S. 1999. *Merging curriculum design with chemical epistemology: A case of teaching and learning chemistry through modeling.* Ph.D. diss., Vanderbilt University.

Grandy, R. 1997. Constructivism and objectivity: Disentangling metaphysics from pedagogy. *Science and Education* 6 (1, 2): 43–53.

Krajcik, J., P. Blumenfeld, R. Marx, and E. Soloway. 1994. A collaborative model for helping teachers learning project-based instruction. *Elementary School Journal* 94(5): 483–98.

Lansdown, B., P. Blackwood, and P. Brandwein. 1971. *Teaching elementary science: Through investigation and colloquium.* New York: Harcourt Brace Jovanovich.

Lehrer, R., and L. Schauble, eds. 2002. *Investigating real data in the classroom: Expanding children's understanding of math and science.* New York: Teachers College Press.

Linn, M., and S. Hsi. 2000. *Computers, teachers, peers: Science learning partners.* Mahwah, NJ: Lawrence Erlbaum.

Magnani, L., and N. Nersessian, eds. 1999. *Model-based reasoning in scientific discovery.* New York: Kluwer Academic/Plenum.

Metz, K. 1998. Scientific inquiry within reach of young children. In *International Handbook of Science Education*, eds. B. Fraser and K. Tobin, 81–96. London: Kluwer Academic.

Millar, R., J. Leach, and J. Osborne, eds. 2001. *Improving science education: The contribution of research.* Philadelphia: Open University Press.

Minstrell, J., and E. van Zee, eds. 2000. *Inquiring into inquiry learning and teaching in science.* Washington, DC: American Association for the Advancement of Science.

National Research Council (NRC). 1996. *National science education standards.* Washington, DC: National Academy Press (*http://www.nap.edu*).

———. 2000. *Inquiry and the national science education standards.* Washington, DC: National Academy Press (*http://www.nap.edu*).

Osborne, R., and P. Freyberg. 1985. *Learning in science: The implications of children's science.* Auckland, New Zealand: Heinemann.

Pellegrino, J., G. Baxter, and R. Glaser. 1999. Addressing the "two discipline" problem: Linking theories of cognition and learning with assessment and instructional practice. In *Review of research in education* (Volume 24), eds. A. Iran-Nejad and P. D. Pearson, 307–53. Washington, DC: American Educational Research Association.

Pellegrino, J., J. Chudowsky, and R. Glaser, eds. 2001. *Knowing what students know: The science and design of educational assessment.* Washington, DC: National Academy Press (*http://www.nap.edu*).

Schauble, L., G. Leinhardt, and L. Martin. 1997. A framework for organizing a cumulative research agenda in informal learning contexts. *Journal of Museum Education* 22(2, 3): 3–11.

Schauble, L., R. Glaser, R. Duschl, S. Schulze, and J. John. 1995. Students' understanding of the objectives and procedures of experimentation in the science classroom. *The Journal of the Learning Sciences* 4(2): 131–66.

White, R., and R. Gunstone. 1992. *Probing understanding.* London: Falmer Press.

Using Questioning to Assess and Foster Student Thinking

Jim Minstrell and Emily van Zee

Jim Minstrell taught science and mathematics for thirty-one years in the public schools, retiring from teaching in 1993. For over twenty-five years he has also conducted research on learning and teaching in his own classroom and the classrooms of many teacher colleagues. He continues doing research and development on assessment of understanding and skills, professional development of teachers, and evaluation of educational programs. He and his colleagues build technical tools to help teachers monitor students' thinking in science and mathematics.

Emily van Zee is an associate professor of science education at the University of Maryland, College Park. She has taught middle school science, contributed to the development of physics curricula, and assisted in physics programs for teachers. She conducted her postdoctoral research in Jim Minstrell's high school physics classroom. Currently she is collaborating with teachers in the development of case studies of science learning and teaching. Her research has focused on student and teacher questioning during conversations about science.

The National Science Education Standards recommend that teachers shift emphasis from assessing memorization of information to assessing scientific understanding, reasoning, and utilization of knowledge (NRC 1996, 82). This shift in emphasis underlies Teaching Standard B: "Teachers of science guide and facilitate learning. In doing this, teachers … orchestrate discourse among students about scientific ideas" (NRC 1996, 32). A key aspect of such discourse is appropriate questioning.

In many science classrooms, questioning typically involves a three-turn exchange in which the teacher asks a question, a student answers, and the teacher evaluates the answer. Student questions are rarely heard in such classrooms. In too many classes, teachers exercise the traditional authority of their position to get students to accept "the" answer rather than engaging students in a reasoned discussion of issues and ideas. One alternative is to involve students in extended conversations. Rather than trying to elicit the "right" answer, teachers can use questioning to elicit student thinking, to find out what conceptions and ways of reasoning their students are using.

A shift toward ongoing assessment involves teachers in establishing norms of scientific argumentation in their classrooms. Scientific argumentation involves knowing how to generate new knowledge from observations and being able to trace the reasoning through which we go from our observations to our conclusions and beyond. Knowing *how* we know is at least as important as knowing *what* we know. Ongoing assessment through the use of different sorts of questions can help guide learners through their thinking. One way to use questioning for ongoing assessment is to ask questions, first to diagnose the state of students' thinking and then to prescribe an appropriate next step to guide students toward a deeper understanding. A comment from one of the students captures the philosophy of this approach to instruction: "Seems like I have to think about everything and understand about everything in order to take another step further."

In this chapter, we first present and discuss an example of using questioning to assess and foster student thinking through a class discussion. The lesson is drawn from a videotape of one of the authors' (JM) high school physics classes. After building a context for questions in the first part, we will summarize some of the sorts of questions that are recommended for ongoing assessment of students' understanding, reasoning, and use of knowledge. Finally we will use an example from the experience of one of the authors to show how results of assessment can be used to guide the adaptation of curriculum and instruction in the classroom.

A Context: Example of Ongoing Assessment through Questioning

Sometimes even successful science students maintain two separate systems for interpreting natural phenomena—what they themselves believe and what they have memorized as the accepted view. The lesson described here was a "benchmark lesson" whose purpose was to help students "make sense" of formal representations of physical systems by enlarging their own ways of thinking (diSessa and Minstrell 1998). The conceptual underpinnings of an early version of this lesson have been described elsewhere by the first author (Minstrell 1982).

The lesson began with an ungraded diagnostic question to elicit students' thinking about forces and proceeded through a series of episodes initiated by questions from the students as well as the teacher. This is an example of an exploration of conceptual understanding in which the teacher followed the students' lead in thinking.

Elicitation Questions

Elicitation questions serve several functions. They provide an opportunity for students to articulate the conceptions and reasoning with which they begin their study of a particular topic. They highlight central issues in the upcoming unit and alert students to what they should be thinking about in the days ahead. Often the elicitation questions and follow-up class discussions involve demonstrations that enable students to view physical phenomena more carefully than they may have previously. The follow-up discussions are designed to enable students to examine contexts within which their intuitions are valid and to recognize contexts within which they may need to modify their thinking. By providing the opportunity to articulate their initial conceptions and to clarify these ideas, the elicitation questions and subsequent discussions help students begin building new, more powerful conceptions.

An elicitation question on forces is shown in Figure 1a. The question asks students, individually at first, to identify the forces acting upon a book that is lying on a table and to draw and label their representation of the force(s) acting in that situation. In typical responses, a vertical arrow pointing downward represents the gravitational force exerted on the book by the Earth, as shown in Figure 1b. However, in about half the papers no upward force is shown. A response more consistent with the view of scientists is shown in Figure 1c, which represents an upward force by the table, balancing the downward force exerted on the book by the Earth.

Figure 1a. Elicitation Question Related to Forces on a Book at Rest

A book is at rest on a table.

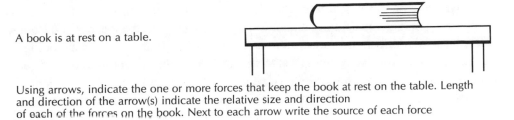

Using arrows, indicate the one or more forces that keep the book at rest on the table. Length and direction of the arrow(s) indicate the relative size and direction of each of the forces on the book. Next to each arrow write the source of each force (i.e., force by _____).

Figure 1b. Typical Student Response to Elicitation Question in Figure 1a.

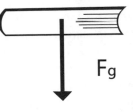

Figure 1c. Typical Scientists' Response to Elicitation Question in Figure 1a.

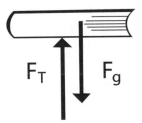

Many students begin the study of force with the idea that only animate objects are capable of exerting forces, that the table cannot exert an upward force on the book because it is not able to push actively on the book. The elicitation question and subsequent discussion help students recognize that an active agent is not necessary, that inanimate objects can passively exert forces such as the upward force on a book by a table. We believe that such issues must be explicitly addressed if we want students to "make sense" for themselves of ways in which scientists understand and represent the world.

Questioning Episodes

The following is an edited transcript of a videotaped, follow-up lesson on forces; it shows highlights of a discussion that typically requires about 30–45 minutes to conduct. We have partially annotated the transcript below with comments that discuss what is happening conceptually and/or linguistically through the teacher and student utterances. We divided the transcript into seven episodes that involve questioning by the teacher and/or students: invitation to students to speak, student initiation of questioning, student comparison of beliefs, negotiation of meaning between student and teacher, class poll, group demonstration, and summarizing mini-lecture.

Episode 1: Invitation to students to speak. In the first episode, Minstrell repeated a statement made by one of the students as a way to invite other students to participate in the discussion:

Teacher: *Does it make sense to everybody that the table is exerting an upward force on that book?* [four-second pause] *No? OK. Want to argue against it?*

Students should actively engage in thinking about an idea until they can articulate reasoning that "makes sense" to them. The long pause gave students time to think about the issue and to venture a response (Rowe 1974). By the questioning "No?", Minstrell reflected back his interpretation of the students' nonverbal responses, that there were some for whom this did not make sense. "OK. Want to argue against it?" invited students to express their own ideas if they were in conflict with what another student had stated. Such discussions encourage students to think about issues central to scientific literacy, such as "Why do I believe this?" and "How do I know it?" (Arons 1983).

Episode 2: Student initiation of questioning. One of the students accepted her teacher's invitation. She sought identification of the force by wondering about the reasons leading to that identification:

Sue: *Well, what force is it? I don't understand why that would be a force.*

T: *Why that would be a force?*

Sue: *Why ... what force would it be?*

T: *The force exerted by the table? [repeating what some of the other students had expressed]*

Sue: *Other than just keeping it up?*

The question marks in the last two utterances indicate a rising intonation that we interpret as a question. These contingent responses may be direct echoes or clarifications as in this episode, or they may involve a more complex paraphrase of the student's thought. Such contingent responses seem to help students continue to elaborate their thinking.

Episode 3: Teacher use of questioning to prompt student comparison of beliefs. Minstrell then solicited comments from another student:

T: *What do others of you think? What do you think? Mary?*

Mary: *Well, I think it's got to be exerting some sort of force, maybe it's just a force, kinda resistance, 'cause, I mean, if it wasn't there, it would fall to the ground. So there's got to be something [keeping it up].*

Sue: *How can a table have a force? I mean I understand it's holding the book up, but I don't think there's any force that's ....*

Dan: *It's just matter.*

The teacher uses another question to probe for and clarify the present meaning of force to these students.

T: *How are you conceiving of force that's different from the way some of the other people are conceiving of force?*

Sue: *I guess, well, I don't know, a force is when, well, I would think, I mean, like pushing a book, that's a force, but actually the table's not pushing the book up. I mean, it's just there. It's keeping it from falling down.*

T: *OK.*

Episode 4: Negotiation of meaning between student and teacher. The student continued with a question that offered a rationale for doubting the conception stated by another student and reiterated by the teacher:

Sue: *It's not ... how can it have a force if it's not even doing anything?*

T: *All right. So the table's not doing something.*

Sue: *It's holding it up.*

T: *It's just there.*

Sue: *It's not like pushing it up. It's just there, so it's not falling.*

T: *OK.*

Notice that the teacher is assessing and reflecting students' ideas and not evaluating them. By saying "OK," Minstrell is acknowledging that he thinks he is understanding what the student means. Then, another student offered an assessment of what makes the concept of force difficult:

Ann: *Like Sue said, a lot of people's conception of a force and mine too is something active, like pushing or pulling, or something that can be proven like gravity, or something like that, but it's hard to conceive of something just kind of being there as exerting a force. I mean it's hard to, like when people think of forces, like lifting or something, but the table's not lifting it, but you know there has to be something there, else it will fall to the ground.*

Episode 5: Class poll to assess current thinking.

T: *OK. So how many of you, at this point, are really struggling with or questioning the idea of whether or not we want to think of something like the table as exerting an upward force?* [Nearly half of the students raise their hands.] *OK. So several of you are still wrestling with that.*

By polling the class periodically during the discussion, Minstrell structured classroom events in a way that explicitly recognized the process of learning. Polling the class prompted students to acknowledge their current point of view and to monitor changes in their conceptions during the discussion.

Episode 6: Group demonstration. Minstrell used a demonstration to establish an "anchor" (Clement, Brown, and Zeitsman 1989; Camp and Clement 1994) in a context that students could understand, an upward force on the book by the hand. He then used this anchor to build a bridge toward a new understanding:

T: *Bill, would you hold your hand out like that please?* [puts book on student's outstretched hand] *How 'bout in that situation?* [students laugh as teacher brings a high stack of books and places them on the student's outstretched hand] *What about that? Do you think, is Bill exerting a force?*

In a next sequence not included here, the teacher places the book on a spring that gets compressed. The students then point out that while the spring is not alive it is flexible. They ask, "What would happen with a solid, really stiff thing supporting the book?" The book is put on the demonstration table and a light beam is aimed at a low glancing angle off the tabletop to the far wall. The spot of light moves slightly when the heavy book is placed on or taken off the table. Again the teacher is anchoring from the spring to the table so that the table acts as a "very stiff spring." All through this sequence the teacher is posing situations that prompt questions from the students. Then the teacher presents situations that guide students to answer their own questions. The sequence of questions and demonstrations proceeds along a line of questioning that forms a context in which the teacher can now summarize the development of ideas, why scientists say that even passive objects like tables can exert forces.

Episode 7: Summarizing mini-lecture. At this point, Minstrell inserted a mini-lecture, a brief exposition by the teacher that summarized the thinking so far and emphasized the bridging connection that Minstrell hoped the students would make between the various situations.

> **T:** *The question is whether we should also say that there is a force exerted by the table. Now the physicist wanting to come up with a logical sort of definition for force that makes rational sense as you go across different situations says, "Look, I see something in common in these situations. This book* [on the hand] *is at rest. So, if I want to say that here the book is at rest and what keeps it at rest is a down force exerted by the Earth and an up force exerted by the hand, and those two balance each other, well, shoot, I guess that means that I better think of force as something that the table can do as well. But I want to think of that as sort of a passive support that the table does rather than as something really active muscular wise. If I want to be logical about it, then I want the same kind of explanation here* [points to diagram of book on table] *as what I have over here* [points to diagram of book on hand]*."*

In a follow-up interview, Minstrell explained what he was trying to do through the set of episodes.

> *Part of what we're trying to do in this activity is to focus on the pattern recognition side of problem-solving or situation-solving.... So in this set of episodes, we were essentially looking at the book on the table and bringing up*

lots of issues out of that, and then we looked at the book on the hand and that one was easy to understand for us, that the hand was exerting an upward force, but can tables do that? Here, the important piece is that students then begin looking at the patterns and saying, "Well, wait a minute … just like the hand supports the book, something's got to be supporting the book when it's on the table, so the table's supporting the book, although passively, so we end up concluding that our definition of force might best include passive sorts of action." The "at rest" becomes an important pattern—it's "at rest" on the table or it's "at rest" on the hand or it's "at rest" on a spring; these are all "at rest" and "at rest" becomes the pattern that we're recognizing … not whether it's on the hand or on the table but the fact that it's "at rest" wherever it happens to be. Understanding the pattern of balanced forces in an "at rest" situation prepares students for distinguishing later between two frequently confused situations: an object "at rest" and a tossed ball at the top of its arc, which is not "at rest" even though its velocity is zero at one instant.

We use the term *reflective discourse* to represent the above type of classroom interaction (van Zee and Minstrell 1997; van Zee et al. 2001). Reflective discourse describes classroom interaction in which students as well as teachers are actively engaged in monitoring their own and others' thinking. We have defined reflective discourse to be classroom talk in which (1) students typically express their own thoughts in comments and questions rather than reciting textbook knowledge, (2) the teacher and an individual student often engage in an extended series of questioning exchanges, and (3) student-student exchanges sometimes involve one student trying to understand the thinking of another. As discussed below, we have identified several kinds of questions that occur during reflective discourse. "In addition to optimal wait-time, it [questioning strategy] requires a solid understanding of the subject matter, attentive consideration of each student's remarks, as well as skillful crafting of further leading questions" (Atkin, Black, and Coffey 2001, 35).

Purposes and Kinds of Questions Used in Learning Science

The central purpose of questioning is to ask or promote the asking of questions that foster deep understanding rather than questions that ask for repetition of memorized information and conclusions. For each sort of question described below, we will give an example related to the discussion above and follow with a few other typical examples focused on that questioning purpose. The readers are encouraged to think of other questions they have used that are consistent with each sort of question listed.

1. Ask or promote questions to open an inquiry and elicit students' initial understanding and reasoning. The elicitation question just prior to Episode 1 in the first part of this chapter asked students about the forces on a book on the table, even before they had studied that situation or topic. "Even though we have not yet studied this topic formally, I want to know what ideas you have at this point in time. You will not be graded on whether you are right or wrong. That is not the point of this exercise. Use words and diagrams to answer the question 'What force or forces would be acting on the book while it is at rest on the table?' Briefly explain how you decided."

2. Ask or promote questions to interpret and make sense of data in order to generate new knowledge and understanding. In Episode 7 the teacher is modeling the sort of thinking and questioning of oneself that he wants students to do as they attempt to make sense of the results of their investigations. Examples of these sorts of questions include the following: "In what ways are all these situations the same? How might I explain all of them the same way?" "Look at the data you generated. What patterns or relationships do you see in the data?" "What can you conclude from your observations?"

3. Ask or promote questions to clarify or elaborate on observations and inferences. If students are not encouraged to be clear in their verbal expression of ideas, there may be a tendency for the teacher to think the student has the same understanding as the teacher or another student and the speaking student may get an invalid assessment. In Episode 3 the teacher asked for clarification: "How are you conceiving of force that's different from the way some of the other people are conceiving of force?" Another more general form of questioning for clarification or elaboration is, "Say more—can you be more specific about what you observed? What did you see in the container as each new chemical was added?" Also, teachers and students need to clarify terms that have been used—for example, "What do you mean by the term _____ which you just used?"

4. Ask or promote questions to encourage learners to justify their answers and conclusions or to explain their reasoning to go beyond a mere stating of an answer. An example is in Episode 3 when Sue asked, "How can a table have [exert] a force?" Other examples of asking for justification include the following: "Why do you think that variable will increase?" "Briefly explain how you decided that would happen?" "How do you know?" "Why do you believe [that conclusion]?"

5. Ask or promote questions to extend or apply learned ideas. Since the context above was to develop new understanding, there are no examples of applying what has been learned, but after Episode 7 such a question could have been asked—for example, "Given the argument I just summarized, how would you apply those ideas to the forces acting on a person sleeping on a mattress as compared with a person sleeping on a cement patio?" Other examples of application questions include the following: "Given the relationship we just concluded, what would happen to the output variable if we doubled this input variable?" "What are some other situations in which you think this idea might apply? Say how it applies." "What would happen if …?"

6. Ask or promote questions that help learners monitor their own learning. In Episode 1 the teacher asked, "Does it make sense to everybody that the table is exerting an upward force on that book? No? Want to argue against it?" Other examples of promoting the monitoring of learning include the following: "So, how have your ideas changed as a result of our activities of the past class period [past week]?" "What do you not yet understand? What doesn't make sense to you yet?" "What would you need to do to test your idea (or answer your question)?"

Although the sorts of questions above are listed separately, many questions will have dual purposes. For example, a particular question may ask students to clarify their ideas, while at the same time asking for justification of knowledge. These are the sorts of questions that can help teachers assess student's ability to reason and learn from experiences as well as assessing their science content knowledge. The questions could be used either in verbal interaction with individual students or with whole classes, and most could also be used in written assessments of students, such as in quizzes or in focused writing in journals.

Using Questions and Answers to Inform Instruction

Listening to or reading students' responses to questions gives assessment information that can inform instruction. This part of the chapter will be in first person by the first author, whose experience is described here.

Early in my teaching I did not address students' thinking. For example, I taught about explaining the "at rest" state of objects by demonstrating with a cart that if I pushed horizontally in one direction on the cart, the cart would move (accelerate) unless I also pushed with an equal force on the cart in the other direction with my other hand. This situation was completely consistent with the students' belief that forces can be exerted by active objects. I fear that many of my students never did learn why we believe that even passive objects can exert force.

Later, when I engaged in action research in my classroom, I became more interested in and responsive to learners and adjusted my instruction to their needs. Based on what I learned from research about the problematic aspects of their ideas and reasoning, I chose or adapted lessons to address their ideas and promote a deeper understanding. Since there were almost no curricular resources that specifically addressed student thinking, I needed to adapt lessons, often on the fly. The lesson described in this chapter is one of those lessons. I will describe here how what I was learning through assessment was changing what I did in the classroom.

From the pre-instruction elicitation question I knew that about half the class believed that passive objects didn't exert force. I wanted to find some situation in which they believed there would be an upward support force, a situation in which they might see similarities with the book on the table. I chose the book on the outstretched hand. Even in this case students wanted to know if the hand was actually outstretched or whether the person was sleeping with his or her hand resting on a table, in which case they didn't think the person would be exerting a force. So the person was awake in my supposed situation of the book on the outstretched hand.

Since many of their explanations involved saying that the difference was that the person was active, that the person was alive, I searched my mind for a situation in which there was an obviously active object that was not alive. That was when I thought of using the spring. I asked about the forces exerted by the spring. The feedback from students suggested that they believed that while the spring was not active, one could readily see that the spring was affected by the book. So, they seemed to give up on the "live" aspect but remained tied to the need for some recognizable "activity" of the object that was supporting the book. They were convinced that the rigidity of the table did not reveal any level of "activity."

Armed with this information about their thinking, I again searched my mind for a way to show that the table was acting like a spring, that is, that the table could flex as well. The very sturdy demonstration table I was using to demonstrate the book on the table did have a shiny surface. Somehow I thought of glancing a light beam off the tabletop. I hoped to use the tabletop as a "light lever." I set the light beam at a low angle so it would reflect off the tabletop to the far wall. I put the book on the table but the movement was too small to be noticeable by the whole class. So, I sent one student to the wall to tape a piece of paper on the wall where the light was hitting. Then after marking where the edge of the light beam hit the paper without the book on the table, I put the book on the table and the student observer noted that the beam moved ever so slightly. I then climbed onto the table so the whole class could see the movement of the beam. It was noticeable to everyone. I was more like the stack of books.

From this series of situations the students themselves concluded that the table was acting "like a very stiff spring." They had moved from believing that only live objects could exert force to active objects (that show deformation) exerting force to the view that even rigid objects like tables could deform and exert force.

There were still a few students who continued to object, saying that "if the support object was very solid [rigid] like concrete or rock, there would be no deformation and therefore no force." I again searched my mind for evidence they could see of concrete or rock deforming under stress. I pulled out a piece of video of the Tacoma Narrows Bridge Collapse, which has a segment showing the concrete roadway of the bridge flexing and deforming in undulating wave patterns shortly before it broke apart and fell into the water below. By now virtually all the students were willing to hold tentatively true that all support structures, whether active or passive, could exert force. The structures just showed it differently.

Now this whole sequence of assessment questions, discussion, and activities has become part of my teaching curriculum and that of teachers with whom I work. Thus, results of assessment can inform instruction and result in improved learning. This and similar assessment tasks and related lesson activities can be found at *http://www.talariainc.com/facet* (click on Diagnoser Tools).

Summary

Assessment can be ongoing with daily class activities such as elicitation activities, discussions, demonstrations, and lab activities as well as quizzes and tests. The sorts of questions that can reveal the most information are questions that ask for deep thinking, that will elicit explication of understanding and reasoning. Finally, the results of assessment can inform instructional decisions.

One final point is very important: The use of these sorts of questions for ongoing assessment and use of the assessment results for redirecting curriculum and instruction can be stimulating professionally. When in the classroom, I now wear two hats, one as a teacher and another as a researcher studying my students' thinking and how to effect better learning. I can no longer teach without learning about my students' thinking. The more I learn about my students' thinking, the more I can tune my instruction to help students bridge from their initial ideas toward more formal scientific thinking. One of my teacher colleagues put it this way: "I used to think only about the activities I was assigning to students. I now have to think about what is going on in my students' heads and then think about what I need to do as a teacher to challenge problematic thinking and promote deeper thinking. I go home each day tired out but energized about the improved effects I am having." Rather than merely serving students the activities from the book, we are first using questions to diagnose their thinking. Then, we choose activities to address their thinking. Thinking in this way about our work in the interest of improving our practice is part of what it means to be professional. Teaching never becomes boring—quite the contrary. As teachers, we can expect to be lifelong learners about our profession.

Acknowledgments

We are indebted to Professor Gerry Philipsen of the Department of Speech Communication at the University of Washington for suggesting the term *reflective discourse* to describe the ways of speaking that we recount in this chapter. A special thanks to our teacher colleagues who have allowed us to work with them, shoulder to shoulder, to better understand teaching and learning.

The research reported in this chapter was supported by grants from the James S. McDonnell Foundation Program in Cognitive Studies for Educational Practice. Preparation of this chapter was partially supported by grants from the National Science Foundation.

References

Arons, A. 1983. Achieving wider scientific literacy. *Daedalus* 2: 91-122.

Atkin J. M., P. Black, and J. Coffey, eds. 2001. *Classroom assessment and the national science education standards*. Washington, DC: National Academy Press.

Bransford, J. D., A. L. Brown, R. R. Cocking, eds. 1999. *How people learn: Brain, mind, experience, and school*. Washington, DC: National Academy Press.

Camp, C., and J. Clement. 1994. *Preconceptions in mechanics: Lessons dealing with students' conceptual difficulties*. Dubuque: Kendall Hunt.

Clement, J., D. E. Brown, and A. Zeitsman. 1989. *Not all preconceptions are misconceptions: Finding "anchoring conceptions" for grounding instruction on students' intuitions*. Paper presented at the annual meeting of the American Educational Research Association, San Francisco, CA.

diSessa, A., and J. Minstrell. 1998. Cultivating conceptual change with benchmark lessons. In *Thinking practices in mathematics and science learning*, eds. J. Greeno and S. Goldman. Mahwah, NJ: Lawrence Erlbaum.

Minstrell, J. 1982. Explaining the "at rest" condition of an object. *Physics Teacher* 20(1):10–14.

———. 2001. The role of the teacher in making sense of classroom experiences and effecting better learning. In *Cognition and instruction: 25 years of progress*, eds. D. Klahr and S. Carver. Mahwah, NJ: Lawrence Erlbaum.

National Research Council (NRC). 1996. *National science education standards*. Washington, DC: National Academy Press.

Rowe, M. 1974. Relation of wait-time and rewards to the development of language, logic and fate control. Part one: Wait-time. *Journal of Research in Science Teaching* 11(2): 81–94.

van Zee, E., and J. Minstrell. 1997. Reflective discourse: Developing shared understanding in a physics classroom. *International Journal of Science Education* 19: 209–28.

van Zee, E., M. Iwasyk, A. Kurose, D. Simpson, and J. Wild. 2001. Student and teacher questioning during conversations about science. *Journal of Research in Science Teaching* 38: 159–90.

Involving Students in Assessment

Janet E. Coffey

Janet Coffey currently works with middle school science teachers on the Classroom Assessment Project to Improve Teaching and Learning (CAPITAL), a National Science Foundation–funded effort that seeks to better understand the assessment practices of teachers and teacher change in the dimension of assessment. She is particularly interested in students' roles and perspectives in assessment activity and the intersections of assessment and learning, both in and out of school settings. She is a former middle school science teacher, worked at the National Research Council as a staff memeber on the development of the National Science Education Standards, and holds a Ph.D. in science education from Stanford University.

"Does anybody have any suggestions or comments?" asked Allison, a sixth grader, at the end of a presentation of her investigation of the growth rate of tomato plants given varying amounts of fertilizer.

"I like the way you described photosynthesis on the poster, and you explained the data well. I still don't understand what in the fertilizer affects the growth. How come more wouldn't be better?" was one reply from a classmate. Another student commented on her eye contact with the audience and suggested she use a louder voice when sharing her observations and data. Subsequent comments pertained to presentation of data, level of detail in her observations, and the model she provided of her design setup. Mark complimented Allison on the manner in which she organized her data and decided that he could present his own data in a similar manner for his study on rates of erosion. The teacher asked Allison to explain how she designed her experiment and if new questions arose in the process of her investigation.

After this class discussion, students completed a written evaluation of the presentation, and the teacher provided feedback as well. Allison completed a written reflection on her final product—what she had accomplished, what she learned, what questions still lingered with her, and what she would do differently next time. Allison would have ample opportunity to consider the feedback from her peers and teacher before she completed her next investigation, project, or presentation.

In the vignette above, we see students actively engage in assessment-related activities—deliberating about quality work, reflecting on and revising work, completing evaluation sheets, and commenting on work done by their peers. In some form or another, planned or unplanned, students have opportunities to participate in many of these types of activities every day, yet these types of exchanges and interactions are often not what first comes to mind when we think of assessment. Assessment is often thought of as an event or strategy—a test, a performance activity, a portfolio, a response to a specific item. Whether it comes after teaching, while teaching, or by teaching, we often think of assessment as something done *to* students, not *with* them. These common conceptions of assessment obscure the roots of the word: "to assess" derives from the Latin *assidere*, "to sit with." Students engaged in and involved with assessment reflect the term's origins. As well, they represent a classroom assessment culture that is supportive of student learning.

This chapter addresses the student in the realm of everyday assessment. After a brief consideration of the research literature, I discuss a middle school science program that prioritized student involvement in assessment. A closer look at the program illuminates some of the supports that may help students as they become more involved in their own assessment and as they learn the skills necessary to incorporate assessment into their everyday learning. The chapter concludes with suggestions about opportunities that exist for students to participate meaningfully in assessment.

Locating Students in Assessment Activity

From gauging student understanding to assigning grades, from planning the next set of questions to communicating to parents, teachers use assessment for a wide range of purposes, not the least of which is the support of student learning. Teachers

- check assignments and interpret student responses,

- listen closely to students' questions so that they can gain insight into their students' understandings,

- seek to make explicit the assessment criteria so that all students know how they will be evaluated,

- try to use what they learn through assessment to inform teaching, plan future learning activities, and provide relevant feedback,

- constantly gauge trends in class engagement, interests, and understandings, and

- strive to fairly assign grades that accurately reflect what a student knows and is able to do.

While all of these responsibilities certainly are important dimensions of effective teaching, ways in which students themselves can participate in assessment are less clear.

Everyday assessment is a dynamic classroom activity that includes the ongoing interactions among teachers *and* students as well as more scheduled events, such as weekly quizzes and unit tests. Attention to student involvement, then, becomes a necessary aspect of assessment activity. Considered broadly, assessment encompasses all activity wherein the quality of work or behavior is discussed, reflected upon, examined, or established. In any classroom, students participate in an assessment activity whenever they are involved in the examination of *quality* of work—whether or not the teacher guides this activity and whether or not the focus is on actual student work or on examples the teacher provides. The form this participation takes varies enormously. Class discussions can center on what makes a piece of work good, what could be improved, and what attributes students can use to improve their own work. Student assessment also occurs when

- students appropriate an idea they saw in another class that made a presentation compelling to them.

- they reflect on what they are learning, how it fits into a bigger picture, what they still do not understand, and where they can seek extra help.

- they consider the thoroughness of their responses to test questions while they are taking a test and when they review their graded exam as a class.

- they make a case to their teacher about why their response deserves more points than she initially assigned.

While these types of activities occur with great regularity in many classrooms, the nature and quality of the experience are worthy of deliberate attention and consideration.

One of the many purposes of everyday assessment is to facilitate student learning, not just measure what students have learned. As we note in the literature, key features of assessment that improve student learning include explicating clear criteria (Butler and Neuman 1995), improving regular questioning (Fairbrother, Dillon, and Gill 1995), providing quality feedback (Kluger and DeNisi 1996; Bangert-Drowns et al. 1991), and encouraging student self-assessment (Sadler 1989; Wolf et al. 1991). The importance of student involvement in assessment, the fourth feature, needs to be underscored. While teachers can do much to assist their students, ultimately, the student must take action (Black and Wiliam 1998). A teacher cannot learn for a student. She cannot participate in activities in place of her students and expect her students to benefit. When students play a key role in the assessment process they acquire the tools they need to take responsibility for their own learning.

Research literature supports the idea of explicitly engaging students in assessment. In a controlled study conducted by White and Frederiksen (1998), for example, four middle school science classes received the same inquiry-based instruction and were given criteria for expectations and grading. Two of the classes used time during class to regularly reflect on what they were learning and how they were learning it (including using evidence from their work to support their evaluations). The other two classes, the control classes, spent the same amount of time talking about how the curricular activities could be modified. Although criteria were made available to all four classes, the two experimental classes that spent time involved in assessment-related discussions about learning performed better on project work and on the unit test. Lower-performing students (as designated by their scores on the California Test of Basic Skills) in the experimental class showed the greatest improvement in performance when compared to the control class. In light of the National Science Education Standards' (NRC 1996) underlying principle that science teaching and programs should support all students in their quest for high performance in science, the improvement seen across all levels in the experimental group is significant.

Benefits of student participation in assessment are varied and far-reaching and ultimately can contribute to improved student learning, as the study described above suggests. Other advantages exist as well, perhaps related to or contributing to these improved learning outcomes. Participation in assessment provides students with opportunities to discuss, contribute to, and develop an explicit understanding of what constitutes quality work. In the process of such deliberation, students often generate many of the salient educational goals themselves (Duschl and Gitomer 1997), which can increase their commitment to achieving them (Dweck 1986). Participating in assessment can also provide students with opportunities to reflect on what they are learning in order to make coherent connections within and between subject matters (Resnick and Resnick 1991). Brown (1994) stresses the strategic element of being aware of particular strengths and weaknesses: "Effective learners operate best when they have insight into their own strengths and weaknesses and access to their own repertoires of strategies for learning" (9). To become a self-directed, lifelong learner, an aim set forth in the *National Science Education Standards* (NRC 1996), the ability to self-assess becomes essential. A closer look at a program in which middle school students participated in assessment shows how students can become involved in assessment and benefit from doing so.

Learning from Connections

The scene of Allison and her classmates that opens this chapter represents a typical scene in Connections,[1] a middle school program that sought to engage students in assessment as a meaningful part of their everyday classroom experiences. Assessment of work was an explicit part of students' classroom activity—doing it, talking about it, learning how to use it to improve their work. Assessment-relevant conversations about public displays of student work, student reflections, peer evaluations, goal setting, teacher and peer observations, and tests were everyday occurrences in the program (Coffey 2002).

Through the students' explicit participation in all aspects of assessment activity, they arrived at shared meanings of quality work. Teachers and students used assessment to construct the bigger picture of an area of study, concept, or subject matter

---

[1] Connections is a semi-contained sixth-, seventh-, and eighth-grade program that sits within a large public middle school in the San Francisco Bay Area. The students take many of their core academic classes within Connections and join their peers from the larger school for electives, such as music, physical education, art, and foreign languages. The eighth-grade students also take math and science with their peers from the larger school. The author conducted extensive research in Connections classrooms and is greatly indebted to the Institute for Research on Learning, formerly in Menlo Park, California, for funding the study.

area. Student participation in assessment also enabled students to take greater responsibility and direction for their own learning.

Shared Meanings of Quality Work

One of the benefits of student participation in assessment is the emergence of a shared understanding among all of the students of what constitutes quality work. Rather than remain as a tacit understanding of teachers, or of savvy students who have figured out expectations, when criteria become explicit, all students understand what it takes to do "good" work. In any classroom, criteria for good work come from somewhere. In Connections, they were informed by standards in the field and workplace, by district guidelines, by years of the teachers' experiences, as well as by student experience, observations, and reflections about what looks and sounds good in the work they produce and share in the classroom. With roots in all of these, students and teachers negotiated what became high-quality work in these classrooms—sometimes explicitly but often implicitly.

The conversation that Allison and her classmates had following her presentation on the effects of fertilizer and the other activities that ensued highlight some of the ways that this idea of quality became established. Let's take a closer look at the vignette that starts this chapter.

Allison's presentation allowed her classmates to observe her organization, representation, and explanation of data, and it allowed her to share with her classmates what she had learned about plant growth. She also discussed her research design and possible areas for further study. Following her presentation, students offered ideas about what they liked (e.g., her description of photosynthesis) and what they thought she could have done differently (e.g., speak in a louder voice). They also asked for clarification, such as regarding the role that fertilizer plays in plant growth. Comments about what her classmates thought was good—and their explanations of why they thought this way—were heard and evaluated by everyone in the class. Likewise, the teacher's comments and questions focused attention on a certain area or set of issues. Allison received feedback, as did the other students who observed her work and followed the conversation.

All of the observations were not made public. Students could note something they liked, or even didn't like, and address those aspects in their own work. Mark made note of her effective organization and display of data, which gave him ideas for his own work. Written evaluations afforded students opportunity for further reflection on the quality of work they had just observed and provided Allison with additional feedback. In this case, Allison developed the written evaluation sheet the students completed for her work as part of the assignment. In the process of constructing the evaluation sheet, she reviewed key areas that were important for feedback. She thought about questions to ask with regard to key ideas and, reflecting on her explanations for the results, realized she still needed to consider other factors that could have influenced growth besides the amount of fertilizer. The teacher's comments addressed the key areas Allison included on her sheet as well as ones the teacher thought were worthwhile. She focused most of her remarks on content, an aspect of the presentation in which students were not as confident in their comments. All of the feedback could be considered and, if appropriate, incorporated into Allison's next piece of work. As work in this class improved, in part due to deeper understandings of what makes something high-quality work, the starting point for these conversations shifted.

These activities were not unique to this assignment. From the start of the year, Allison, her classmates, and the teacher engaged in discussions about work, about what makes something good, about what they liked, about what they thought could be improved. In September, reflective conversations about work were established as a class norm. Furthermore, students had numerous opportunities to observe and reflect on work prior to Allison's presentation, and they understood that they would have numerous opportunities to engage in similar assignments in the future.

No single activity led to shared meanings of what constitutes quality work. These meanings emerged in a number of ways, including from

- students generating their own evaluation sheets,

- conversations in which students and teachers shared ideas about what constituted a salient scientific response, or a good presentation, lab investigation, or project,

- discussions of an actual piece of student work,

- students' reflections on their own work or a community exemplar, and

- students' decision making as they completed a project.

These meanings were reinforced and revised as students evaluated their own and others' projects, used their new understanding to inform a piece of work, and adopted a common way of talking about work with peers.

Detailed and in-depth understandings of quality did not appear immediately, nor were they static. With frequent reflection and discussion, Connections students' ideas of what constituted a good project became more refined over time; ideas among students began to converge. Conversations and comments evolved along with understandings of the criteria. Initially, students' reflections and comments on their own and their peers' work focused primarily on process and presentation-related aspects of work. We see some of these types of comments in the opening example, when students respond to Allison's request for feedback with remarks about her eye contact and suggestions that she speak louder. Eventually, students improved in these areas and less explicit attention was directed to them.

Gradually, with direction from the teacher, issues related to science content moved to the foreground of reflection and discussion. Here, too, ideas evolved. While most students know content is an important dimension of good work, particular aspects of content that are important can take time to develop. In Connections, students began to remark more frequently on content issues, such as clarity of information, organization of information, source of information, and even accuracy of information. In the opening vignette with Allison, we see evidence of this shift. One student's remark, for example, indicated that she did not understand the relationship between fertilizer and plant growth. This remark also suggested that while students were listening to their peers, they were reflecting on their understanding. This had not always been the case in September. Another student's comment accented the level of detail in Allison's observations. Over the course of the year, students learned to ask questions about evidence and explanation. Inclusion of "key ideas" and major concepts as goals for what content to include and convey gradually replaced "a lot of facts."

A shared idea of what makes good work developed in Connections through explicit attention to issues of quality in all stages of assessment and work. Even when the teacher introduced criteria from the outside, such as in the form of a rubric, criteria needed to be discussed and negotiated in order to become understood by and operational for all students. A rubric the teacher distributed for a library research assignment on erosion, for example, indicated that the top "score" of "5" required that students include at least five facts about soil types. Many students spent time counting the number of facts, without a real sense of why five facts were better than four facts for this particular assignment or how to make the facts hang together for a more convincing argument. On a related assignment, a rubric indicated to students that a "5" required them to write a "clear hypothesis" for an investigation on absorption rates for soil samples. Many of the students did not know what constituted "clear" for a hypothesis and only developed a notion of "clear" after class discussions and numerous examples. In short, providing the students guidelines or criteria for evaluation did not replace the need for an iterative process of meaning making that happened by explicitly attending to what makes good work—during day-to-day work and before, during, and after project development and presentation.

Developing understandings of quality takes time and is an iterative and collaborative process. Discussions do not end with a rubric or grading scale; they are ongoing and evolving, and become increasingly sophisticated with time and practice. When a class has shared definitions and standards for good work, students can more effectively participate in an activity, as well as in the assessment of their own work and that of others.

Assessment as a Means to Connect to a Bigger Picture

Relationships and interrelationships between and among ideas, concepts, and activities are not always clear, especially early in a unit or at the beginning stages of an investigation. Yet, an aspect of understanding a subject area or concept involves coming to understand the relationships between what may appear as seemingly disparate practices, activities, and information. For students in Connections, participation in assessment helped forge these connections and establish a broader framework for what they were learning.

Take, for example, a test review for the seventh-graders' unit on the cell. Part of the test review entailed a discussion comparing the parts of a cell, and the functions of those parts, to different parts of a submarine. For some students, this culminating exercise helped to establish the relationship between the parts and the whole. Organelles and their functions were considered together and in relationship to each other, and discussion included the whole class. Although the teacher had attempted to build in this broader framework throughout the unit, some students needed the final review in order to truly make sense of what they had been learning. Another aspect of the test review entailed small groups of students writing test questions, some of which the teacher would use on the actual exam. These small-group discussions served as further review (and helped to demystify the origins of test questions). After the test was returned, the class went over their responses as a class, and students had an opportunity to do test corrections for a homework assignment. In this case, the activities that occurred before and after the test were as important for learning as the actual test itself. Conversations about the students' presentations of their investigations, of which Allison's is just one in a series, provided other opportunities to do much more than simply hear what classmates have been up to. The class discussed fundamental aspects of science as a practice, such as communication of data, information, and conclusions. Students came to see that communication is an intrinsic aspect of scientific endeavors.

Opportunities to reflect, both as individuals and as a group, helped improve students' understandings and made clearer how what they were doing connected to a broader topic or idea and, at times, to a larger world of science. Coupled with reflection, assessment-relevant conversation and activities gave students the opportunity to synthesize information and experiences; the revision process helped them to clarify criteria and to strengthen connections and analysis. Establishing a bigger picture was a collaborative endeavor: Class discussions and shared reflections, for example, allowed students access to connections others had made and provided data for teachers about student learning. Making these connections explicit and the bigger picture more apparent is particularly important in terms of reaching all students.

Assessment as a Vehicle to Facilitate Lifelong Learning

One aspect of becoming more self-directed in an activity involves identifying what is not well understood. Learning is no exception. An important feature of participation is knowing when and where to go to for additional, and perhaps more expert, help. The relationship between learning and assessment, particularly the timing of assessment, changed in Connections, as students became intimately involved in the assessment process. The role assessment played in the actual doing of the project work changed, too. By the end of the school year, for example, seventh graders used assessment as a way of seeing whether they needed to gather more data, whether they had provided an adequate explanation of their data, and whether their conclusions mapped back to their hypotheses. In the process of making her evaluation sheet, and reflecting on key questions to ask, Allison recognized that she needed to revise her own explanations about what happened. As students read material, they paused to reflect on the main points, and as they listened to the presentation of material, they reflected on their understanding, as was the case with the student who asked Allison about fertilizer. As they planned investigations, they made sure their initial questions were clear. Assessment shifted from something that largely followed learning—measuring what had been learned—to something that occurred simultaneously with learning. This came to occur with such fluidity that the two became inextricable and difficult to tease apart. For many students, assessment became a vehicle for asking questions that would help clarify their understanding and help guide production of good work. Students became more self-directed in their assessment as they learned what questions to ask and what questions they should be able to answer.

Reflection became incorporated into the students' everyday classroom activities, whether prompted by the teacher, a peer, or themselves. In the busy lives of students and schools, carving out the time for quiet reflection can be somewhat difficult, but students grew to appreciate its value. As one seventh grader said, "When you think about what you learn, you actually learn it. It soaks in more."

Relationship among Students, Content, and Assessment

In response to a teacher's request to reflect on certain subject matter, a student may ask, "How can I assess what I don't know?" Students are not the only ones who hold this view. When teachers design ways to involve students in assessments, they may overlook involvement in the content dimensions of work on the same premise—that students will not be able to evaluate the accuracy of specific information. Relationships among content, assessment, and students become critical issues as teachers shift some of the responsibility for assessment to students. A trade-off, and some would say tension, exists in involving students in the assessment of their work in the realm of content.

With time and an increasingly clear idea about what is important to consider with respect to content, students can become more *self-directed* with respect to assessing content. Questions about evidence and sources can guide work, reflection, and revision. Students can learn to look for, and ask themselves and each other about, main points and key concepts. If students ask themselves questions such as, "What is the evidence?", "What do we know?", "How do we know it?", and "Where does this information come from?"—and if they pay attention to their subsequent responses—they are becoming familiar with their own understanding of the content, and they can move on to ask questions about their peers' understanding. They can develop a better sense of when they do not really understand something and, importantly, when to look for information as well as where and to whom to go for that information.

Although students may learn to consider content, and develop tools for doing so, they still may not be able to evaluate the soundness or accuracy of an explanation on, say, photosynthesis. Teachers play an important role in involving students actively in assessment, but the challenges associated with involvement are not obstacles that cannot be overcome. Assessment-relevant conversations related to content help cultivate within students the types of questions they should be asking when dealing with content information. In addition to commenting on content in terms of accuracy and soundness, teachers can facilitate conversations related to content, highlighting aspects of content and asking questions about it in their own remarks.

Creating Meaningful Opportunities for Assessment

If students are to take greater responsibility for their own learning and assessment, they must be afforded opportunities to participate meaningfully in assessment. The Connections program offered lessons in six areas about how to organize and support student participation.

1. Time. Involving students in assessment activity takes time. Teachers in the Connections program prioritized assessment as an important activity by providing time and opportunities for students to participate. They traded time from other teaching activities so students could *do* assessment. They guided and provided scaffolding for student involvement. They contributed their own feedback and determined when their remarks were most relevant and when to back off to let student contributions carry more weight. Students, likewise, invested time and energy into providing feedback to peers, commenting on work, contributing to assessment conversations, and reflecting on work.

2. Use of Traditional Assessment. Many of the assessment opportunities in Connections arose in exchanges among students and teachers and between and around the more visible assessment events. A student's presentation or a test, and episodes preceding and following these events, provided opportunities for the class to discuss and establish aspects of quality work, to establish the role that assessment would play in the classroom, to generate the norms and guiding assessment principles that operate in the classroom, and to use criteria to inform work in process.

Teacher and students leveraged test review as an opportunity to return to the bigger picture of what they had been studying. The class talked about what was going to be covered on the test or quiz so that all students knew what to expect. For some, these discussions provided opportunities to make connections, if they had not been made before. Discussions about tests also served as springboards to talk about the meaning of assessment. The test process also encompassed graded responses after the test, and students would often do test corrections after going over the test. On occasion students would write test questions and grade their own work.

3. Public Displays of Work. During the initial weeks and months of school, teachers used public displays of student work to catalyze conversations about good work, to prompt student reflection, and to promote peer feedback. At times, work done by a student from a previous year or work done by a teacher or another adult served as the basis of these conversations. Immediately following presentations of work, teachers asked students to consider what was successful and effective and what could be improved and how. Such discussions about quality of work and suggestions for improvement were established as a classroom norm. Gradually teachers asked students to provide written evaluations on work. These written evaluations augmented the discussions and provided additional opportunities to cultivate and support reflection, as well as additional avenues for feedback.

4. Reflection. Teachers asked students to reflect on dimensions that should be included in upcoming work. They asked for volunteers to share thoughts publicly. These conversations often addressed general features to consider in a piece of work or presentation; they also offered students the opportunity to think systematically about quality and about their own work with respect to quality. The class reflected, both publicly and privately, after doing their work. Gradually, students were encouraged to reflect during work as well. The integration of reflection into daily practice helped students grasp "the big picture."

5. Revision. Students had opportunities (and expectations) to revise their work. They did this with peers and teachers as they went along, submitting proposals and meeting to discuss their progress. Often the teacher would request that a student redo something, taking into account the feedback that he or she had received.

6. Goal Setting. Another dimension of the assessment activities involved goal setting. Students set short- and long-term goals and specific and broad goals. Throughout the year, they reflected on progress made toward these goals and set new goals. For project work, daily and weekly goals helped students to prioritize big ideas and to keep themselves focused during work time. By reflecting on progress toward their goals, students considered their current work in light of where they were headed. With time and attention, the teacher could help students increase the specificity of their goals in different subject areas. Longer-term goals served as the centerpiece of student-led student-teacher-parent conferences.

Learning to Assess and Learning How to Use Assessment

At times, especially early in the school year, opportunities to participate in self-assessment were not immediately embraced. Students would ask questions like, "Isn't this your job?" when asked to reflect on their progress. Students resisted requests for written reflection on their work and struggled to come up with evidence for accomplishments or progress. And when they did participate in class discussions, student contributions tended to be incomplete and at times even superficial. At the start of the year, students had difficulty identifying key components of a good lab report, essay, or response.

The quality of student participation in assessment improved in Connections as students learned and practiced the necessary skills to participate meaningfully. With a teacher's help, students learned how to reflect on work, both for a single occasion and on work over time; they learned how to comment constructively on peers' work; they learned what constituted quality work; they learned how to use assessment in ways that informed their work in process. Students became better at assessing as they had opportunities to assess. Despite initial resistance, as students learned assessment-related skills, demarcations between roles and responsibilities with respect to assessment blurred. They learned to take on responsibilities and many even appropriated ongoing assessment into their regular habits and repertoires.

Conclusion

To create a culture of assessment that promotes powerful and productive student learning, the roles students play in the assessment process need to be re-examined. Their essential role in the process—as partners, not just as recipients—needs to be recognized. Numerous opportunities exist for students to participate, but they need to be supported in their efforts to do so.

With support and guidance from the teacher, student involvement can grow and build over the course of the year. As students learn how to participate, their involvement shifts to become more integrated and self-directed. High levels of student involvement take time and investment, on the part of both teacher and students, and will not happen overnight. Any single assessment event or episode cannot be isolated from the whole of the activity. Student engagement with and participation in any one event seeps into and informs the others. Student-developed evaluation sheets, as well as responses, for example, are informed by ongoing deliberations about what constitutes quality work.

Lessons from Connections and the research literature show that cultivating a productive assessment culture becomes compelling. As students learn to engage in and with assessment, assessment can be incorporated into everyday work habits, not just at the urging of the teacher, but as a productive and inextricable dimension of learning, and these habits can extend well beyond the school walls.

References

Bangert-Drowns, R. L., C-L Kulik, J. A. Kulik, and M. T. Morgan. 1991. The instructional effect of feedback in test-like events. *Review of Educational Research* 61 (2): 213–38.

Black, P., and D. Wiliam. 1998. *Inside the black box: Raising standards through classroom assessment.* London: King's College. Also published in *Phi Delta Kappan* (1998) 80 (Oct.): 139–48.

Brown, A. L. 1994. The advancement of learning. *Educational Researcher* 23 (8): 4–12.

Butler, R., and O. Neuman. 1995. Effects of task and ego-achievement goals on help-seeking behaviours and attitudes. *Journal of Educational Psychology* 87 (2): 261–71.

Coffey, J. E. 2002. *Making connections: Students engaging in and with assessment.* Doctoral diss., Stanford University.

Duschl, R. D., and D. H. Gitomer. 1997. Strategies and challenges to changing the focus of assessment and instruction in science classrooms. *Educational Assessment* 4 (1): 37–73.

Dweck, C. S. 1986. Motivational processes affecting learning. *American Psychologist,* Special issue: Psychological science and education 41 (10): 1040–48.

Fairbrother, B., J. Dillon, and G. Gill. 1995. Assessment at Key Stage 3: Teachers' attitudes and practices. *British Journal of Curriculum and Assessment* 5 (3): 25–31.

Kluger, A. N., and A. DeNisi. 1996. The effects of feedback interventions on performance: A histori-cal review, a meta-analysis, and a preliminary feedback intervention theory. *Psychological Bulletin* 119 (2): 254–84.

National Research Council (NRC). 1996. *National science education standards.* Washington, DC: National Academy Press.

Resnick, L. B, and D. P. Resnick. 1991. Assessing the thinking curriculum: New tools for educa-tional reform. In *Changing assessments: Alternative views of aptitude, achievement and instruc-tion,* ed. B. Gifford. Boston, MA: Kluwer.

Sadler, R. 1989. Formative assessment and the design of instructional systems. *Instructional Science* 18: 119–44.

White, B. Y., and J. R. Frederiksen. 1998. Inquiry, modeling and meta cognition: Making science accessible to all students. *Cognition and Instruction* 16 (1): 3–118.

Wolf, D., J. Bixby, J. Glen III, and H. Gardner. 1991. To use their minds well: Investigating new forms of student assessment. *Review of Research in Education* 17: 31–74.

Reporting Progress to Parents and Others: Beyond Grades

Mark Wilson and Kathleen Scalise

Mark Wilson is a professor of education at the University of California, Berkeley, specializing in educational assessment, educational evaluation, and applied statistics. He holds a B.Sc. (mathematics), teaching certificate (elementary education), and master's degree (research methodology) from the University of Melbourne. He completed a Ph.D. in measurement from the University of Chicago. Extensively published in professional journals and books, his work involves (a) the development of new psychometric models for analyzing student performance in theory-rich contexts such as complex performance assessments and intelligent tutoring systems, (b) the application of current measurement theory to practical problems of testing and evaluation, and (c) the development of assessment resources that are useful to classroom teachers, policy makers, and other education professionals.

Kathleen Scalise is a Ph.D. student in quantitative measurement at the University of California, Berkeley. She was the science writer for the high school physics, chemistry, biology/life sciences, and Earth sciences chapters of the 2002 California Science Framework for K–12 Public Schools, produced by the Curriculum Frameworks and Instructional Resources Division of the California Department of Education. She holds a bachelor's degree in biochemistry from the University of California, Berkeley, and holds teaching credentials in both physical and life sciences.

When it comes to grades and grading practices in the United States, there is one thing parents often don't understand and students understand all too well: Getting an A, B, or C, even passing or failing a class, is often based more on a teacher's perceptions of a student's effort than on accomplishment.

This "secret of current classroom grading," said one middle school teacher during a recent online gripe session, "frustrates many teachers as they think about holding students to high standards. It's hard to be tough about standards when a student says to you, 'But I tried so hard.' But we've got to help teachers get past this, because we all deal with the repercussions when we judge students mostly on effort" (Berry 1997).

What are the repercussions when such grades, and only such grades, are reported to parents and students as the final summation of success in a class? Students think, as would be expected, that they have satisfied course objectives to the extent of the grade and so do their parents, assuming the grade is based on mastery of content, strategies, or other learning goals that may not have been met at all. Later when students encounter more challenging work for which they are not prepared, failure sits on their shoulders as a lack of ability, talent, or some other hard to quantify but definitely personal characteristic; surely it cannot be lack of preparation when they have done so well in prerequisites.

A single score in the form of a grade can do little to inform mastery of today's complex science standards, consisting of multiple strands and numerous objectives. Add to this the confounding effect of incorporating effort, work ethics, and other concerns into a grade, on a basis that differs from class to class, and such a score can be all but meaningless in terms of the "rigorous and wise diagnostic information" (Wolf et al. 1991, 31) called for by educators. In the end, when students are trained to work hard but not effectively, and standards are taught but not met, damage can be inflicted on students' opportunities and on their perceptions of themselves and their abilities.

Grades, however, have a long tradition of being awarded on the basis of many considerations and not outcomes alone. Surely the final value judgment of a student's performance in a class should consider many dimensions, including, but not limited to, outcomes. Teachers as experts in their disciplines have long had jurisdiction to set a suitable balance of factors in awarding grades.

And so we see our grading practices have left us perched in a difficult position: What is to be valued and what isn't, and how does any of this relate to standards-based education or any type of education in which learning goals are considered important to assess and communicate?

We argue here that both sides of this grading dilemma can be satisfied. If teachers and students were given robust but easy-to-use tools for generating solid diagnostic information and relating this information to standards or learning goals, they then would have the power to better understand progress toward achievement. Teachers could retain the freedom to decide how to value this information toward assigning a grade. Parents and students could share in diagnostic information while also getting feedback on the larger classroom picture in the form of a grade.

In this chapter, we will discuss the principles of constructing classroom-based assessment tools that can generate high-quality and interpretable evidence for teachers, students, and parents, and we show how these tools can be built into curriculum materials. A new "embedded assessment" system designed at the University of California, Berkeley, called the BEAR Assessment System (Wilson and Sloane 2000), will be introduced as a generic approach that can be customized to the needs of many courses. The system was named for its origin at the Berkeley Evaluation and Assessment Research (BEAR) Center and is a comprehensive, integrated system for assessing, interpreting, and monitoring student performance. It provides a set of tools for teachers and students to use to

- reliably assess performance on central concepts and skills in a curriculum,

- set standards of performance,

- validly track progress over the year on the central concepts, and

- provide feedback on student progress and effectiveness of instructional materials and approaches for teachers, students, parents, administrators, and other audiences.

A Word about Embedded Assessment

The term *embedded assessment* means what it says: assessment activities are "embedded," or become part of, classroom learning activities, indistinguishable from day-to-day operations. Teachers have been doing embedded assessment for a long time: a homework assignment, for example, is embedded assessment, as are a lab practical, a classroom discussion in which students first jot down their thoughts on the topics, and a short-answer essay. Any of these and much more can be considered an embedded assessment activity if a student produces something that can be scored or rated or if the student can be observed and assessed in some manner. The only difference between these examples and what we discuss here as more formal embedded assessment is that the latter calls for attention to task design and formal "calibration" of assessment tasks in relationship to a framework that describes the learning to take place and that can be used to generate interpretable, valid, and reliable diagnostic information on student performance.

We argue that embedded assessment is desirable not only because it reflects what a student is actually being taught but also because it can be a learning tool in and of itself. If an assessment task is also a learning activity, then it does not take unnecessary time away from instruction, *and* the number of assessment tasks can be increased in order to improve the results of measurement, diagnostics, and accountability (Linn and Baker 1996).

The potential usefulness of embedded assessments can be greatly enhanced when the framework on which they are based is consistent with that for the more formal assessments used in accountability assessments, such as school district or state assessments. This also greatly enhances the value of the more formal assessments (for a discussion of this point, under the topic "assessment nets," see Wilson and Adams 1996).

What Is Needed in an Assessment System: Four Principles

With the accountability debate raging, it is hard to imagine principles of assessment that would be widely agreed upon by all. However, a few central concepts seem to stand out. Here we first develop and then address four principles that we believe any assessment system designed to be useful in the classroom must uphold: a developmental perspective, the generating of quality evidence, a match between instruction and assessment, and management by teachers.

Principle 1: A Developmental Perspective

A developmental perspective of student learning means assessing the development of student understanding of particular concepts and skills over time, as opposed to, for instance, making a single measurement at some final or supposedly significant time point. Traditional classroom assessment strongly supports a developmental perspective. Every teacher knows he or she must make repeated measurements of student progress, often done with tests and quizzes, as instruction proceeds. Standardized testing situations and educational research, however, often neglect this perspective. "One-shot" testing situations and cross-sectional approaches—comparing two sets of students at different times as if they were one set proceeding from one time to the next—abound in education. Here we affirm what is perhaps the obvious: For diagnostic information to be diagnostic, it must be collected over time and in relationship to some set of goals about what is to be learned.

However obvious, it is important to emphasize this perspective because of its logical implications. To truly understand and interpret the significance of development requires a *model* of how to interpret data taken at these repeated intervals. Clear definitions of what students are expected to learn, and a theoretical framework of how that learning is expected to unfold as the student progresses through the instructional material, are necessary elements to a well-grounded developmental perspective.

Principle 2: Quality Evidence

For classroom-based assessment procedures to gain "currency" in the assessment community, issues of technical quality have to be addressed. Despite criticism of standardized tests based on issues such as the impoverished nature of questions and the often poor match between instructional goals and what is assessed, standardized tests are based on extensive background and technical work on issues such as reliability—the reproducibility of results—and validity—measuring what is intended to be measured. Standardized exams also are vetted for bad questions; in addition, they are tested prior to use and their interpretability is enhanced by being normed.

These issues have typically been ignored in classroom-based assessment until now. Despite the plea of Wolf et al. (1991), the development of practical procedures for establishing the technical quality of classroom-based assessments lags far behind high-stakes assessment programs. To ensure comparability of results across time and context, these issues must be addressed in any serious attempt at a developmental assessment system for use in the classroom.

Additionally, classroom-based assessments should maintain standards of fairness, such as consistency and absence of bias. If "open-ended" or "performance-based" tasks are used, for instance, they require procedures to ensure fairness and consistency of scoring (as well as fairness and consistency in collecting and managing student work). Responses can no longer be scanned by machine and entered directly into a database. Raters score the work, and besides fairness this also raises issues of time and cost.

It is a long-accepted truism that teacher-made (i.e., "classroom-based") student assessments have greater "curricular" or instructional validity—that is, they relate more to actual learning aims—than standardized tests but that they do not have the strong technical properties of carefully constructed standardized assessments. We assert that classroom-based diagnostic assessments must have both. While teachers will and should continue to construct "teacher-made tests" despite not having the opportunity to establish the comparability or validity of these tests, appropriate classroom-based assessment procedures can and should be developed on the basis of educational standards and made available for teacher use and adaptation.

Principle 3: Match between Instruction and Assessment

The third principle of assessment is establishing a good match between what is taught and what is assessed. Reports abound of teachers interrupting their regular curricular materials in order to "teach the material" students will encounter on district- or state-wide tests. Traditional testing practices—in high-stakes or standardized tests *as well as* teacher-made tests—have long been criticized for using too many questions that assess only memorized facts and ignore more complex levels of understanding. As Resnick and Resnick (1992) argued, "Assessments must be designed so that when teachers do the natural thing—that is, prepare their students to perform well—they will exercise the kinds of abilities and develop the kinds of skill and knowledge that are the real goals of educational reform" (39). Assessments that don't meet the goals of instruction fail this test.

Principle 4: Management by Teachers

This final principle is perhaps most critical: Classroom-based assessment systems must be under the jurisdiction of teachers. Teachers must be the managers of the system. They must have the tools to use the system efficiently and to explain resulting data effectively and appropriately. Students must also be able to participate in the assessment process, and they should be encouraged to develop essential metacognitive skills that will further the learning process.

There are two broad issues involved in this principle. First, it is the teachers and students who will use the assessment information to inform and guide the teaching and learning process. By the very nature of turnaround time, assessments conducted as part of district- or statewide accountability programs—no matter how valid or appropriate to what is taught in the classroom they may or may not be—cannot provide the immediate feedback that teachers and students need for instructional management and monitoring (Haney 1991; Resnick and Resnick 1992). For this function of assessment, teachers and students must be

- involved in the process of collecting and selecting work for assessment,

- able to score and use the results immediately, not wait months for scores to be returned,

- able to interpret the results in instructional terms, and

- able to have a creative role in the way assessment is realized in their classrooms.

Second, issues of teacher professionalism and teacher accountability demand that teachers play a central and active role in collecting and interpreting evidence of student progress and performance (Tucker 1991). If teachers and students are to be held accountable for performance, they need a good understanding of what students are expected to learn *and* of what counts as adequate evidence of student learning. Teachers are then in a better position, and a more central and responsible position, for presenting, explaining, analyzing, and defending their students' performances and outcomes of their instruction. Students are better able to develop their own metacognitive skills and to bring them to bear in the learning process.

This perspective requires new views of the teaching and learning process, new roles for and demands on teachers, perhaps even a new "assessment culture" in the classroom (Brown et al. 1992; Cole 1991; Resnick and Resnick 1992; Torrance 1995a, 1995b; Zessoules and Gardner 1991). Preparing teachers and students to use these types of assessments in the classroom may be a difficult challenge. But we should recognize that teacher understanding and belief in assessment often will determine the ultimate success of change (Airasian 1988; Stake 1991).

The BEAR Approach

An assessment approach that can meet the tests of these principles while remaining adaptable to the needs of each course in which it may be used is challenging to design. A number of different approaches might work. Here we present solutions developed through our work with science curriculum developers and embodied in the BEAR Assessment System (for more detail, see Wilson and Sloane 2000).

Satisfying Principle 1: A Developmental Perspective

Our strategy to address this issue is to develop a set of "progress variables" (Masters, Adams, and Wilson 1990; Wilson 1990) that mediate between the level of detail that is present in the content of specific curricula and the necessarily more vague contents of state standards and curriculum framework documents. These progress variables are the core of the generic assessment system that we have developed to help teachers make the best use of the information contained in assessments. Progress variables define the intended content of a specific curriculum up to a level of detail that would allow, say, biweekly tracking of student progress through the curriculum. These variables define the most important student growth goals of the curriculum; the variables change from course to course as different areas of knowledge are assessed.

Every instructional unit is seen as contributing in some way to student progress on at least one of these variables, and every assessment is closely aligned with one or more of these variables. This alignment allows the creation of a calibrated scale to map the growth of students, so that teachers can track the progress of individual students and groups of students as they engage in learning and instruction. This idea of a "cross-walk between standards and assessments" has also been suggested by Eva Baker (Land 1997, 6). These variables create a "conceptual basis" for relating the curriculum to standards documents and to other curricula.

In this approach, the idea of a progress variable is focused on the concept of progression or growth. Learning is conceptualized not simply as a matter of acquiring quantitatively *more* knowledge and skills, but as progress toward higher levels of competence as new knowledge is linked to existing knowledge and deeper understandings are developed from and take the place of earlier understandings. The concepts of ordered levels of understanding and direction are fundamental in our approach.

To use the BEAR Assessment System in any given area it is assumed that learning can be described and mapped as progress in the direction of qualitatively richer knowledge, higher-order skills, and deeper understandings.

Variables are derived in part from professional opinion about what constitutes higher and lower levels of performance or competence, but are also informed by empirical research into how students respond to instruction or perform in practice. To more clearly understand what a progress variable is, let us consider an example: progress variables recently designed for a high school chemistry curriculum, "Living by Chemistry: Inquiry-Based Modules for High School" (Claesgens et al. 2002).

The Living by Chemistry (LBC) project at the University of California's Lawrence Hall of Science is a National Science Foundation–funded, yearlong course to teach chemistry using real-world contexts familiar and interesting to students. The course developers were interested in this approach to assessment for at least two reasons. First, they wanted to reinforce the conceptual understanding and problem-solving aspects of the course. Traditional "fact-based" chapter tests would not reinforce these aspects, they believed, and could direct the primary focus of instruction away from the most important course objectives. Second, the developers wanted to explore learning trajectories in high school chemistry, gather reliable data on which curricular approaches best facilitated student learning, and understand for whom these approaches succeeded and failed, and why.

Following the Developmental Perspective principle, we worked with the LBC curriculum development team to devise a framework of progress variables, called "Perspectives of Chemists," that attempt to embody understanding of chemistry from a novice to expert level of sophistication and that incorporate the national and California state science education standards. Three sets of perspectives variables, or strands, were designed to describe chemistry models and views regarding three "big ideas" in chemistry: matter, change, and energy. The *matter* strand is concerned with describing atomic and molecular views of matter, as well as measurements and model refinement regarding matter. *Change* involves kinetic views of change and the conservation of matter during chemical change. *Energy* considers the network of relationships in conservation and quantization of energy.

Each strand consists of an atomic viewpoint on the topic under consideration and a macroscopic, or systems, viewpoint.[1] The LBC framework is shown in Figure 1. While too complex to be considered in full here (see Claesgens et al. 2002 for more details), to illustrate the use of progress variables we will consider assessment data collected on one portion of the framework: the progress variable representing the atomic

---

[1] While for expert chemists the atomic and systems views are integrated into a single perspective, conceptual change literature in chemistry suggests that a major source of misconceptions for novices involves confusion of atomic and systems properties—for instance, considering a molecule of water to be tear-shaped, like a tiny drop of water, and a molecule of ice to have the geometry of an ice cube (Griffiths and Preston 1992).

Figure 1. Perspectives of Chemists

Levels of success	A Visualizing matter ATOMIC AND MOLECULAR VIEWS	B Measuring matter MEASUREMENT AND MODEL REFINEMENT	C Characterizing change REARRANGEMENTS OF ATOMS	D Quantifying change CONSERVATION OF MASS	E Evaluating energies CONSERVATION OF ENERGY	F Quantizing energy QUANTIZATION OF ENERGY
6 Understanding	Bonding and relative reactivity	Models and evidence	Kinetics and changes in bonding	Stoichiometry and equilibrium	Particle and energy views	Spectroscopy and structure
5 Integrating	Phase and composition	Limitations of models	Products of reaction	Amounts of products	Degrees of change	Electronic structure
4 Predicting	Properties and atomic views	Measured amounts of matter	Change and reaction types	Amount of reactants and products	Energy transfer and change	Color with light absorption
3 Relating	Matter with chemical symbols	Mass with a particulate view	Change with chemical symbols	Change with a conservation view	Heat and temperature	Energies associated with light
2 Representing	Properties of matter	Amounts of matter	Attributes of change	Changes in mass	Measures of energy	Light
1 Describing						

Source: Claesgens, J., K. Scalise, K. Draney, M. Wilson, and A. Stacy. 2002. *Perspectives of chemists: A framework to promote conceptual understanding of chemistry.* Paper presented at the annual meeting of the American Educational Research Association, New Orleans.

and molecular view of matter, called "Visualizing Matter." Note that each progress variable was based first on expert opinion of likely progressions of learning and then refined and modified with extensive collection of data, which in this case generated some findings that surprised the developers.

The Visualizing Matter variable incorporates California state science education chemistry standards 1c, d, g; 2a, e, f, g; and 10b, d, e (see Appendix). It shows how a student's view of matter progresses from a continuous, real-world view, to a particulate view accounting for existence of atoms and molecules, and then builds to relate this view to more complex behaviors and properties of matter.

Our assessments with pilot studies of this variable show that a student's atomic views of matter begin with having no atomic view at all, but simply the ability to describe some characteristics of matter, such as differentiating between a gas and a solid on the basis of real-world knowledge of boiling solutions perhaps encountered in food preparation, for instance, or bringing logic and patterning skills to bear on a question of why a salt dissolves. This then became the lowest level of the Visualizing Matter variable in the LBC framework.

At this most novice level of sophistication, students employ no accurate molecular models of chemistry, but a progression in sophistication can be seen from those unable or unwilling to make any relevant observation at all during an assessment task on matter, to those who can make an observation and then follow it with logical reasoning, to those who can extend this reasoning in an attempt to employ actual chemistry knowledge, although incorrectly in first attempts. All these behaviors fall into Level 1, the Describing level of the framework, and are assigned incremental 1- and 1+ scores, which for simplicity of presentation are not shown in this version of the framework.

When students begin to make the transition to accurately using simple molecular chemistry concepts, Level 2 begins, which we call the Representing level. At Level 2 of the Visualizing Matter progress variable, we see students using very one-dimensional models of chemistry: A simple representation, a single definition will be used broadly to account for and interpret chemical phenomena. Students show little ability to combine ideas, but begin to grasp and use simple definitional concepts such as elements, compounds, solutions, and valence electrons.

When students can begin to combine and relate patterns to account for, for instance, the contribution of valence electrons and molecular geometry to dissolving, they are considered to have moved to Level 3, Relating. Remaining levels of the framework represent further sophistications, extensions, and refinements on Level 3 and are not expected to be mastered in high school but in university courses.

This example shows how a progress variable can be developed to generate information on student mastery. It assumes, however, that data collected are quality data, an issue we next address.

Satisfying Principle 2: Quality Evidence

Technical issues of reliability and validity, fairness, consistency, and bias discussed in Principle 2 can quickly sink any attempt to measure along a progress variable as described above. To ensure comparability of results across time and context, procedures are needed to (a) examine the coherence of information gathered using different formats, (b) map student performances onto the progress variables, (c) describe the structural elements of the accountability system—tasks and raters—in terms of the achievement variables, and (d) establish uniform levels of system functioning, in terms of quality control indices such as reliability. While this type of discussion can become very technical to consider, it is sufficient to keep in mind that the traditional elements of test standardization, such as validity and reliability studies and bias and equity studies, must be carried out to satisfy quality control and ensure that evidence can be relied upon.

Our approach on this technical end of measurement is to use item response modeling (also known as IRT), as described by Adams and Wilson (1992, 1996). These are measurement models now well-developed enough for use in classroom-based assessment in a fairly routine and feasible way. The output from these models can be used as quality control information to address the concerns above, and to determine where individual students fall on a progress variable such as Visualizing Matter, or any other progress variable that might be conceived and validated.

The formal nature of these models and their flexibility allow one to address technical challenges inherent in the classroom assessment situation, such as the maintenance of teacher rating consistency and the maintenance of a meaningful scale throughout the school year. This puts richer information into the hands of teachers in the classroom. The central feature is the *progress map*, which provides a graph of the progress that students are making through the curriculum. Shown in Figure 2a and Figure 2b are two maps—one showing one student's progress along the Visualizing Matter variable and the other showing where this same student stands on all four of the LBC high school progress variables. Maps are derived from empirical analyses of student data collected from classrooms.[2]

Once constructed, maps can be used to record and track student progress and to illustrate the skills a student has mastered and those that the student is working on. By placing students' performance on the continuum defined by the map, teachers can demonstrate students' progress with respect to the goals and expectations of the course. The maps, therefore, are one tool to provide feedback on how students as a whole are progressing in the course.

---

[2] These maps were drawn in GradeMap, an experimental software package developed at the University of California, Berkeley (Wilson, Draney, and Kennedy 2002). The analyses for these maps were performed using the ConQuest software (Wu, Adams, and Wilson 1998), which implements an Estimation-Maximization algorithm for the estimation of multidimensional Rasch-type models. For a detailed account of the estimation and model-fitting see Draney and Peres (1998).

Figure 2a. A "Conference Map" for a Single Student

GradeMap				_ □ ×

File

Name: Mary Rodgers

	Visualizing Matter	Measuring Matter	Characterizing Change	Quantifying Change
2+				
2		*		
2-	*			
1+			*	
1				
1-				*
0				
To improve your performance you can:	Review periodic table trends, octet rule, and phase changes. Be careful to answer questions completely, and do not leave out key details.	You will often need to consider two or more aspects of the atomic model when you solve problems. Don't rely on just 1 idea.	Review phase changes and the kinetic view of gases. You need to know more about motions of atoms and molecules.	Keeping track of mass as it reacts or changes form is challenging. Consider the info you are given and be willing to take a best guess.

Note: The map helps the student know where he or she measures on each progress variable and makes suggestions for how the student can improve.

Maps, as graphical representations of student performance on assessment tasks, can be used by teachers for their own instructional planning and to show students, administrators, and parents how students are developing on progress variables over the year. This can then be used to inform instructional planning. For instance, if the class as a whole has not performed well on a variable following a series of assessments, then the teacher might go back and readdress those concepts or issues reflected by the assessments. Additionally, during the development stage, unsatisfactory map results can indicate changes or additions to the curriculum.

Satisfying Principle 3: Match between Instruction and Assessment
The match between the instruction and assessment in the BEAR Assessment System is established and maintained through two major parts of the system: progress variables, described above, and assessment tasks, described in this section. The main motivation for the progress variables so far developed is that they serve as a framework for the assessments and a method of making IRT measurement possible. However, this third principle makes clear that the framework for the assessments and the framework for the curriculum and instruction must be one and the same. This is not to imply that the

Figure 2b. A "Progress Map" for a Single Student on the Visualizing Matter Variable in Two Curriculum Modules (Weather and Toxins)

	GradeMap					_ □ ✕

File

VM	MM	CC	QC

Overall Performance for: Mary Rodgers — **Visualizing Matter**

PRETEST	WEATHER 1ST TIME PT.	WEATHER 2ND TIME PT.	TOXINS	Score	Criterion Zone
				1950	
				1900	
				1850	Level 2+
				1800	
				1750	
				1700	
				1650	Level 2
				1600	
				1550	Level 2-
				1500	
				1450	
				1400	Level 1+
				1350	
				1300	
				1250	Level 1
				1200	
				1150	Level 1-
				1100	
				1050	
					Level 0

Note: The first timepoint is a pretest score, followed by a first and second assessment of the same student in the Weather module and a final assessment in the Toxins module. The horizontal bands represent the score levels of the Visualizing Matter progress variable, calibrated by item response modeling of data from classroom tests of the assessment system completed during curriculum development.

needs of assessment must drive the curriculum, but rather that the two, assessment and instruction, must be in step—they must both be about accomplishing the same thing, the aims of learning, whatever those aims are determined to be.

Using progress variables to structure both instruction and assessment is one way to make sure that the two are in alignment, at least at the planning level. In order to make this alignment concrete, however, the match must also exist at the level of classroom interaction and that is where the nature of the assessment tasks becomes crucial. Assessment tasks need to reflect the range and styles of the instructional practices in the curriculum. They must have a place in the "rhythm" of the instruction, occurring at places where it makes instructional sense to include them, usually where teachers need to see how much progress their students have made on a specific topic (see Minstrell 1998 for an elaboration of such occasions).

One good way to achieve this is to develop both the instructional materials and the assessment tasks at the same time—adapting good instructional sequences to produce assessable responses and developing assessments into full-blown instructional activities. Doing so brings the richness and vibrancy of curriculum development into assessment, and also brings the discipline and hard-headedness of assessment data into the design of instruction.

The variety of assessment tasks used by the BEAR Assessment System can range widely, including individual and group "challenges," data interpretation questions, and tasks involving student reading, laboratory, or interactive exercises. In LBC tasks, all assessment prompts are open-ended, requiring students to fully explain their responses. For the vast majority of assessment tasks, the student responses are in a written format.[3]

An example of an LBC assessment prompt and actual student answers at Levels 1 and 2 are shown in Figure 3. Performance is judged by the validity of the arguments presented, not simply by the conclusions drawn.

By developing assessment tasks as part of curriculum materials, they can be made directly relevant to instruction. Assessment can become indistinguishable from instructional activity, *without precluding the generation of high-quality, comparative, and defensible assessment data on individual students and classes.*

Whatever the form of instruction, if student work is generated or students can be observed at work and this work can be scored and matched to progress variables, then it is possible to consider use of an assessment system such as BEAR and to clearly match the assessments to instruction.

Satisfying Principle 4: Management by Teachers

For information from assessment tasks and BEAR analysis to be useful to teachers and students, it must be couched in terms that are directly related to the instructional goals of the progress variables, and open-ended tasks, if used, must be quickly, readily, and reliably scorable. Our response to these two issues is scoring guides (a.k.a. rubrics). Scoring guides define the performance criteria, or characteristics, for each score level to be awarded. "Living by Chemistry" has one scoring guide used over all variables, with both open-ended tasks scored by teachers and multiple-choice and other close-ended questions scored by machine and computer. Another course might have one scoring guide for each of the progress variables. Thus, decisions on the structure of tasks and deployment of scoring and guides can be made course by course, but must reflect the time constraints and needs of teachers as well as measurement.

---

[3] This is not a limitation of the BEAR system, but reflects the only practical way we had available for teachers to attend to a classroom of student work.

Figure 3. Example of a Living by Chemistry (LBC) Project Assessment Prompt with Actual Student Answers

Question: You are given two liquids. One of the solutions is butyric acid with a molecular formula of $C_4H_8O_2$. The other solution is ethyl acetate with the molecular formula $C_4H_8O_2$. Both of the solutions have the same molecular formulas, but butyric acid smells bad and putrid while ethyl acetate smells good and sweet. Explain why you think these two solutions smell differently.

Student Answers at Level 1 of Visualizing Matter progress variable

Response: "I think there could be a lot of different reasons as to why the two solutions smell differently. One could be that they're different ages, and one has gone bad or is older which changed the smell. Another reason could be that one is cold and one is hot."

Response: "Using chemistry theories, I don't have the faintest idea, but using common knowledge I will say that the producers of the ethyl products add smell to them so that you can tell them apart."

Response: "Just because they have the same molecular formula doesn't mean they are the same substance. Like different races of people: black people, white people. Maybe made of the same stuff but look different."

Analysis: These students use ideas about phenomena they are familiar with from their experience combined with logic/comparative skills to generate a reasonable answer, but do not employ molecular chemistry concepts.

Student Answers at Level 2 of Visualizing Matter progress variable

Response: "They smell differently b/c even though they have the same molecular formula, they have different structural formulas with different arrangements and patterns."

Response: "Butyric acid smells bad. It's an acid and even though they have the same molecular formula but they structure differently."

Analysis: Both responses appropriately cite the principle that molecules with the same formula can have different structures, or arrangements of atoms, within the structure described by the formula. However the first answer shows no attempt and the second answer shows an incomplete attempt to use such principles to describe the simple molecules given in the problem setup, which would have advanced the response to the next level.

Note: To match instruction and assessment, this LBC assessment question followed a laboratory project in which students explored chemicals that had different smells.

When scoring guides are used, teachers and students need concrete examples—which we call "exemplars"—of the rating of student work. Exemplars provide concrete examples of what a teacher might expect from students at varying levels of development along each variable. They are also a resource to understand the rationale of the scoring guides. Actual samples of student work, scored and moderated by teachers who pilot-tested the BEAR Assessment System in a course called "Issues, Evidence, and You," are included with the documentation for the course. These samples illustrate typical responses for each score level for specific assessment activities.

In addition to the scoring guides, the teacher needs a tool to indicate when assessments might take place, and what variables they pertain to. These are called Assessment Blueprints and are a valuable teacher tool for keeping track of when to assess students. Assessment tasks are distributed throughout the course at opportune points for checking and monitoring student performance, and these are indicated in the Assessment Blueprints. Teachers can use these blueprints to review and plan assessment tasks relating to each variable, and to modify the assessments to their own needs.

Bringing It All Together

The four principles of the BEAR system are not designed to operate in isolation. Each of the principles provides a unifying "thread" throughout the system, but their interrelationships also make the system more integrated. For example, the progress variables provide an initial unity to the curriculum materials and define not only the content of student learning but also the paths over which student learning develops throughout the year. The implication is that each assessment, then, has a designated place in the instructional flow, reflecting the type of learning that students are expected to demonstrate at that point in time. Hence, scores assigned to student work can then be linked back to the developmental perspective and used both to diagnose an individual's progress with respect to a given variable and also to "map" student learning over time.

Adherence to each of the principles across each of the phases of the assessment process produces a coherence or "internal consistency" to the system. Adherence to each of the principles within each phase of the assessment process produces a well-integrated system that addresses the complexity of the classroom and desired linkages among curriculum, instruction, and assessment.

Proper operation of the BEAR Assessment System requires that teachers and students "take control" of essential parts of the assessment system, including the scoring process, and also that teachers and students sometimes face demands that they grow in order to master the system. We have devised the "assessment moderation meeting" as part of our staff and student development strategy to accomplish these goals. In these meetings, teachers discuss the scoring, interpretation, and use of student work, and make decisions regarding standards of performance and methods for reliably judging student work related to those standards. Moderation sessions also provide the opportunity for teachers to discuss implications of the assessment for their instruction, for example, by discussing ways to address common student mistakes or difficult concepts in their subsequent instruction. The moderation process gives teachers the responsibility of interpreting the scores given to students' work and allows them to set the standards for acceptable work. Teachers use moderation to adapt their judgments to local conditions. Upon reaching consensus on the interpretations of score levels, teachers can then adjust their individual scores to better reflect the teacher-adapted standards. The use of moderation allows teachers to make judgments about students' scores in a public way with respect to public standards and improves the fairness and consistency of the scores.

Moderation also can take place with student groups, so students can better grasp and determine for themselves what the teacher and course are valuing in terms of student learning. Students can score actual class work, if that is deemed appropriate, or can score work provided as examples in the curriculum materials. They can map scores against progress variables and see more concretely the paths toward mastery of learning aims.

The Bottom Line

An important bottom-line question still remains—does an assessment system make a difference to students' knowledge and mastery of course material and aims? We next consider evidence from a different application of the BEAR Assessment System: the Science Education for Public Understanding Project (SEPUP) at the Lawrence Hall of Science. SEPUP developers created a yearlong, issues-oriented science course for the middle school and junior high grades entitled "Issues, Evidence, and You" (SEPUP 1995). Societal decision-making is a central focus of "Issues, Evidence, and You"(IEY). As part of the course, students are regularly required to recognize scientific evidence and weigh it against other concerns with the goal of making informed choices about relevant contemporary issues or problems.

The "Issues, Evidence, and You" field test took place in the 1994–1995 school year at six centers around the country known as Assessment Development Centers (ADCs). Teachers at these centers were required to use the BEAR Assessment System and to participate in moderation meetings throughout the year; in each of their classrooms, data were collected from the assessment activities. In addition, the study included Professional Development Centers (PDCs), where teachers taught the IEY curriculum and were provided with the same assessment materials as the ADC group *but were not required to use the assessment system.* PDC teachers did, however, participate in professional development activities of similar duration as the moderation activities, related to the curriculum rather than to the assessment system.

In order to examine the effectiveness of the assessment system, the results of the pretests and posttests for the PDC and comparison groups, and the pretests, posttests, and various link tests for the ADC group, were compared. Both groups used the same curriculum. The same instructional and assessment materials were provided to both groups. The only difference in treatment between the two groups was that teachers in the ADC group paid specific attention to the assessment system.

Figure 4 shows that ADC students made substantial gains during the school year, especially as compared with the PDC and comparison students. While the average gain for the PDC and comparison groups was similar (difference not statistically significant at the $p = 0.05$ level), the average gain for the ADC group was significantly greater (3.46 times greater, $p = 0.05$ level).

This gain can also be put in educational terms: The maximum gain for the ADC group is, for the average student, approximately a difference between a 2 and a 3 on the 0–4 scaled scoring guide. Without specific attention to the scoring system, students achieved an average 2 while those under the assessment system evidenced mastery at level 3. This is an educationally significant change, marking a difference

Figure 4. Student Gains in the "Issues, Evidence, and You" Curriculum When Taught by Teachers at Asssessment Development Centers (ADCs), at Professional Development Centers (PDCs), and in a Comparison Group

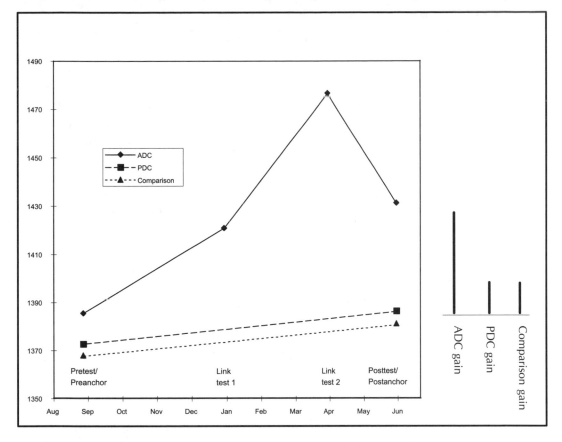

Note: Teachers at ADCs were required to use the BEAR Assessment System and to participate in "moderation meetings" throughout the year. Teachers at PDCs were given the same assessment materials as the ADC group but were not required to use the assessment system. PDC teachers did participate in professional development activities, but unlike the ADC group, the activities were related to the curriculum rather than to the assessment system. Teachers in the comparison group had the embedded items available to them in the student booklet and teacher's guide, but there was no explicit request to use them, or even any encouragement to do so. They did not have the link tests available to them.

between achievement of partial but incomplete success toward the course standards and satisfactory completion.

These results reinforce the common-sense idea that considerable potential gains could be realized by (a) closer attention to assessment concerns at the classroom level and (b) a more systematic approach to the gathering and interpretation of assessment information.

Conclusion

The work reported here takes only a few short steps along some of the paths that could be considered with regard to classroom-based assessment and the generation of high-quality data. It seems clear that going beyond grades to map individual trajectories of learning at the classroom level is feasible, especially as computers and data collection devices become readily available and curriculum is restructured to better accommodate assessment.

In practice, the benefit to students, teachers, and parents is promising. Furthermore, how our theories of learning and theories of instruction may change in science, for instance, as a result of better data out of classrooms and a clearer understanding of learning trajectories is fascinating to consider. We hope to see more formal embedded assessment efforts unfold in coming years, especially in science education as a forerunner in this area, and invite those interested to, of course, consider using the BEAR Assessment System. But, moreover, it is important for educators to ponder the principles behind the system, and that is why we have taken the trouble to lay them out here. It is in satisfying these principles that the argument for classroom-based assessment lies.

"Grades are part of the system and will always be there," said one high school teacher using the BEAR system. "But this kind of analysis gives me more than just a grade. I can diagnose a problem and move forward with a greater number of students. I can see the amount of time it takes for my students to learn, and find out how much of something they know, or how well they know it, not just whether they have a fact in their heads or they don't. It lets me value even wrong answers, because it shows me what in each answer I can value and support and work with. To me, it's a whole different way to truly value student thinking."

Appendix

Science content standards for California public schools covered by the "Living by Chemistry: Inquiry Based Modules for High School" (LBC) Visualizing Matter progress variable include those shown below. Other LBC variables cover the remaining standards.

Grades 9–12—Chemistry

1c. Students know how to use the periodic table to identify alkali metals, alkaline earth metals and transition metals, trends in ionization energy, electronegativity, and the relative sizes of ions and atoms.

1d. Students know how to use the periodic table to determine the number of electrons available for bonding.

1g. Students know how to relate the position of an element in the periodic table to its quantum electron configuration and to its reactivity with other elements in the table.

2a. Students know atoms combine to form molecules by sharing electrons to form covalent or metallic bonds or by exchanging electrons to form ionic bonds.

2e. Students know how to draw Lewis dot structures.

2f. Students know to predict the shape of simple molecules and their polarity from Lewis dot structures.

2g. Students know how electronegativity and ionization energy relate to bond formation.

10b. Students know the bonding characteristics of carbon that result in the formation of a large variety of structures ranging from simple hydrocarbons to complex polymers and biological molecules.

10d. Students know the system for naming the ten simplest linear hydrocarbons and isomers that contain single bonds, simple hydrocarbons with double and triple bonds, and simple molecules that contain a benzene ring.

10e. Students know how to identify the functional groups that form the basis of alcohols, ketones, ethers, amines, esters, aldehydes, and organic acids.

Acknowledgments

The work of the first author was supported by a National Science Foundation (NSF) grant to the CAESL Center, WestEd. The work of the second author and the ChemQuery/Living by Chemistry examples cited in the text were produced and supported by an NSF grant to Professor Angelica Stacy, Department of Chemistry, University of California, Berkeley.

References

Adams, R. J., and M. Wilson. 1992. *A random coefficients multinomial logit: Generalizing Rasch models*. Paper presented at the annual meeting of the American Educational Research Association, San Francisco.

———. 1996. Formulating the Rasch model as a mixed coefficients multinomial logit. In *Objective measurement III: Theory into practice*, eds. G. Engelhard and M. Wilson. Norwood, NJ: Ablex.

Airasian, P. W. 1988. Measurement-driven instruction: A closer look. *Educational Measurement: Issues and Practice* 7(4): 6–11.

Berry, B. 1997. New ways of testing and grading can help students learn and teachers teach. *Reforming Middle Schools and School Systems* 1(2). *http://www.middleweb.com/CSLB2testing.html*.

Brown, A. L., J. C. Campione, L. S. Webber, and K. McGilly. 1992. Interactive learning environments: A new look at assessment and instruction. In *Changing assessments,* eds. B. R. Gifford and M. C. O'Connor, 121–212. Boston: Kluwer.

Claesgens, J., K. Scalise, K. Draney, M. Wilson, and A. Stacy. 2002. *Perspectives of chemists: A framework to promote conceptual understanding of chemistry.* Paper presented at the annual meeting of the American Educational Research Association, New Orleans.

Cole, N. 1991. The impact of science assessment on classroom practice. In *Science assessment in the service of reform,* eds. G. Kulm and S. Malcom, 97–106. Washington, DC: American Association for the Advancement of Science.

Draney, K. D., and D. Peres. 1998. *Unidimensional and multidimensional modeling of complex science assessment data.* BEAR Research Report SA-98-1. Berkeley: University of California.

Griffiths, A. K., and K. R. Preston. 1992. Grade-12 students' misconceptions relating to fundamental characteristics of atoms and molecules. *Journal of Research in Science Teaching* 29(6): 611–28.

Haney, W. 1991. We must take care: Fitting assessments to functions. In *Expanding student assessment,* ed. V. Perrone, 142–63. Alexandria, VA: Association for Supervision and Curriculum Development.

Land, R. 1997. Moving up to complex assessment systems. *Evaluation Comment* 7(1): 1–21.

Linn, R., and E. Baker. 1996. Can performance-based student assessments be psychometrically sound? In *Performance-based student assessment: Challenges and possibilities. Ninety-fifth yearbook of the National Society for the Study of Education,* eds. J. B. Baron and D. P. Wolf, 84–103. Chicago: University of Chicago Press.

Masters, G. N., R. A. Adams, and M. Wilson. 1990. Charting student progress. In *International encyclopedia of education: Research and studies. Supplementary volume 2,* eds. T. Husen and T. N. Postlethwaite, 628–34. Oxford: Pergamon Press.

Minstrell, J. 1998. *Student thinking and related instruction: Creating a facet-based learning environment.* Paper presented at the meeting of the Committee on Foundations of Assessment, Woods Hole, MA (Oct.).

Resnick, L. B., and D. P. Resnick. 1992. Assessing the thinking curriculum: New tools for educational reform. In *Changing assessments,* eds. B. R. Gifford and M. C. O'Connor, 37–76. Boston: Kluwer.

SEPUP. 1995. *Issues, evidence, and you: Teacher's guide.* Berkeley, CA: Lawrence Hall of Science.

Stake, R. 1991. *Advances in program evaluation: Volume 1, Part A: Using assessment policy to reform education.* Greenwich, CT: JAI Press.

Torrance, H. 1995a. The role of assessment in educational reform. In *Evaluating authentic assessment,* ed. H. Torrance, 144–56. Philadelphia: Open University Press.

———.1995b. Teacher involvement in new approaches to assessment. In *Evaluating authentic assessment,* ed. H. Torrance, 44–56. Philadelphia: Open University Press.

Tucker, M. 1991. Why assessment is now issue number one. In *Science assessment in the service of reform,* eds. G. Kulm and S. Malcom, 3–16. Washington, DC: American Association for the Advancement of Science.

Wilson, M. 1990. Measurement of developmental levels. In *International encyclopedia of education: Research and studies. Supplementary volume 2,* eds. T. Husen and T. N. Postlethwaite. Oxford: Pergamon Press.

Wilson, M., and R. J. Adams. 1996. Evaluating progress with alternative assessments: A model for Chapter 1. In *Implementing performance assessment: Promise, problems and challenges,* ed. M. B. Kane. Hillsdale, NJ: Lawrence Erlbaum.

Wilson, M., K. Draney, and C. Kennedy. 2002. GradeMap (Version 2.0) [computer program]. Berkeley: University of California, BEAR Center.

Wilson, M., and K. Sloane. 2000. From principles to practice: An embedded assessment system. *Applied Measurement in Education* 13(2): 181–208.

Wolf, D., J. Bixby, J. Glenn III, and H. Gardner. 1991. To use their minds well: Investigating new forms of student assessment. *Review of Research in Education* 17: 31–74.

Wu, M., R. J. Adams, and M. Wilson. 1998. ACER*ConQuest* [computer program]. Melbourne, Australia: ACER Press.

Zessoules, R., and H. Gardner. 1991. Authentic assessment: Beyond the buzzword and into the classroom. In *Expanding student assessment,* ed. V. Perrone, 47–71. Alexandria, VA: Association for Supervision and Curriculum Development.

Working with Teachers in Assessment-Related Professional Development

Mistilina Sato

Mistilina Sato taught middle school science in New Jersey prior to receiving her doctorate in curriculum and teacher education from Stanford University. She has worked with teachers in a variety of professional development settings on issues such as inquiry and the nature of science; classroom-centered assessment; Earth, space, and environmental sciences; action research; and developing science curriculum. In her current position she works with teachers pursuing National Board Certification and is a research assistant with the Classroom Assessment Project to Improve Teaching and Learning (CAPITAL) at Stanford University. She has been a member of the National Science Teachers Association since 1992.

I begin with a premise about everyday assessment in the classroom: Assessment is inseparable from the instructional practices of the teacher (Atkin, Black, and Coffey 2001). Everyday assessment goes beyond the design of performance assessments administered to students. It is more regularly practiced than the exhibition of culminating classroom projects. It is more tightly bound to instruction than the use of regular quizzes to check students' understanding of discrete concepts. Everyday assessment happens not only every day, but in almost every minute of teacher-student interactions and student-student interactions.

Class discussions, one-on-one interactions with students, and the varieties of student work assigned and collected by the teacher are rife with information about what students are thinking and how well they are performing. Teachers do not always explicitly recognize these interactions as assessment opportunities, that is, as opportunities to use the available information about students' understanding and performance to support student learning. Frequently so much information is available to the teacher that to pay heed to all of it would result in information overload. To use this information effectively for assessment purposes requires that the teacher act upon the information in some way (Sadler 1989). Teachers may use the information to inform their own instructional decisions about the direction of the current lesson or the next concept to address within a curricular unit. Teachers may provide feedback to an individual student or to a group of students as to what they need to do next to continue their progress. Teachers may make note of the information and draw upon it at a later time. Teachers may report the information to parents as a way of demonstrating student progress or suggesting ways that parents can support learning at home.

This ongoing identification, collection, and use of information in the classroom is a complex business. It often requires a shift in the teacher's priorities in the classroom from managing activity and behavior to a mind-set of managing learning opportunities. Traditionally, assessment in the classroom has been viewed as a means by which teachers reach a judgment about the quality of student performances on tests, quizzes, and a variety of classroom projects. Heightening the teacher's awareness about everyday assessment opportunities in the ongoing instruction shifts attention from the products of assessment to the interactions among people in the classroom. Changing assessment practices based on this premise then becomes a matter of change that must incorporate not only new assessment practices, but also a different way of thinking about the role the teacher and students play with regard to assessment. New techniques and strategies for assessing student progress and performance will contribute to improving teachers' assessment practices; however, working with teachers on everyday assessment issues must also address the teachers' views about the assessment cultures in their classrooms.

This chapter looks broadly at approaches to working with teachers on assessment-related matters and highlights an approach that places the teacher as an individual and his or her everyday classroom practices at the center of the professional development interaction. This approach views assessment not only as a means of determining what the students have taken away from instructional interactions, but also as a means of supporting learning as it is taking place. I will not attempt to describe all of the assessment-related professional development work going on around the country. This work is far-reaching, and an essay of this length would not do justice to the various programs and projects. Rather, I will discuss an approach that sees the teacher not only as a professional engaged in learning new ideas or strategies for assessing but also as an individual who is undergoing personal change.

Approaches to Working with Teachers

Work with teachers in assessment-related professional development commonly seeks to introduce teachers to strategies for assessing student performance. In this approach, teachers are taught design principles for creating effective assessments, they examine lesson design to identify when assessment opportunities arise, or they might practice strategies developed by other teachers and consider when these strategies would be appropriate in their own teaching situations.

As other writers in this volume have also pointed out, teachers can examine student work in order to understand what their students know and to refine their assessment. Teachers also can examine the questioning strategies they use in their classrooms and relate the questions posed to the responses offered by students. Dissecting the teacher's practice into discrete elements—such as prompts offered to students in written work or questions posed to students in discussion—helps teachers focus on targeted aspects of their classroom practices. This kind of focused attention allows teachers to learn about, and potentially implement, new techniques.

Experts in the field of assessment have also developed programs for introducing teachers and school organizations to a variety of approaches to classroom assessment and schoolwide systems of assessment. (See, for example, the work of Richard Stiggins, founder of the Assessment Training Institute, an organization in Portland,

Oregon, that offers professional development programs and materials on assessment strategies nationwide [*http://www.assessmentinst.com/index.html*] and the work of Grant Wiggins, president and director of programs for Re: Learning by Design, a not-for-profit educational organization in Pennington, New Jersey, that also consults nationally in professional development and assessment systems [*http://www.relearning.org/*].) In these programs, teachers learn about the technical aspects of assessment design and consider assessment systems that are aligned across grade levels and with the curriculum. These programs intend to help teachers become "literate" in a variety of assessment practices and to become skilled at using them.

In both of these examples, the professional development approach aims to bring about change in the teachers' instructional practice by helping them learn about and implement new assessment strategies, skills, and systems. While there is great need for teachers to develop a stronger understanding about assessment (Stiggins 2002), an approach focused solely on teaching teachers *about* assessment only partially addresses the issue of bringing about change in the teachers' assessment practices.

A teacher's practice comprises more than the technical and strategic moves he or she makes in the classroom. If the classroom is viewed as a place in which teachers deploy a diverse variety of assumptions, theories, and practices, simply introducing teachers to new instructional practices without spending time developing an understanding of the reasons behind the change—and how these changes jibe with the teacher's mind-set about how to operate his or her classroom—may result in the superficial enactment of those practices.

I am reminded of the illustration that David Cohen (1990) offered in his account of "Mrs. Oublier," a second-grade teacher caught up in the reforms in mathematics instruction. In the ongoing efforts to introduce teachers to models of instruction that aligned with the National Council of Teachers of Mathematics' *Curriculum and Evaluation Standards for School Mathematics* (1989), school districts, universities, and standards-based curriculum programs offered professional development opportunities for teachers to help them learn how to teach math using the reform-minded techniques. Mrs. Oublier was observed implementing many of these techniques in her classroom. She was doing what she had learned in the workshops—using manipulatives, engaging the children in multiple modalities for learning, and attempting to draw out deeper meaning about mathematical patterns rather than teaching rote memorization of algorithms. However, based on Cohen's observations, Mrs. Oublier's teaching demonstrated a complex blend of her traditional practices and the new strategies for teaching mathematics. (Cohen represents Mrs. Oublier's practices in an unflattering way, which can be argued to be unfair to the teacher who was actually observed). Based on conversations with Mrs. Oublier, it was clear that she thought that her instructional practices had changed dramatically, shifting toward the reform-minded strategies she had been taught. However, Mrs. Oublier implemented the new techniques filtered through her own traditional teaching experiences and beliefs about what constitutes appropriate responses to mathematics problems, sometimes undermining the desired outcomes of the reform approaches. One can surmise from this example that teachers' experiences and preferences have a great influence on the change process. If change in instructional practices is a desired outcome of professional development, then teaching teachers new techniques and skills is necessary, but not sufficient.

Teachers can be taught a wide variety of new ideas and skills as adult, professional learners. However, teachers do not enter professional development programs as blank slates. The interpretations that teachers bring to new ideas and new roles are bound up with their values, their personal backgrounds, their prior experiences with reform, and their beliefs. Thus, the individual is an inextricable part of how these new ideas and roles are put into action in the workplace. In the next section, I discuss an approach to working with teachers that recognizes the active part that the individual can play in his or her professional development.

A Personal Approach to Working with Teachers

Many factors shape a teacher's pedagogy and, thus, the assessment practices embedded within that pedagogy. The curriculum adopted by a school has embedded assumptions about what should be assessed and, in some cases, how to assess student progress and learning. The conception of the subject matter and its foundational epistemology influence how the teacher selects learning goals, scaffolds lessons aimed at helping students attain those goals, and determines student progress toward those goals. The conception of learning that the teacher holds influences how the teacher designs lessons and how the teacher views the role of student motivation in the learning process. A teacher's practice is also influenced by the established practices within his or her professional community. Finally, teaching can be viewed as a personal act that is guided and shaped by the teacher's prior experiences, preferences, and beliefs.

Teachers' practices comprise a broad range of interactions and decision-making. In the classroom with students, teachers make countless decisions—who to call on in a discussion, when to summarize the main ideas, when to allow a digression. Sanders and McCutcheon (1986) suggest that teachers' decision-making is guided by their practical theories, defined as

> *conceptual structures and visions that provide teachers with reasons for acting as they do, and for choosing the teaching activities and curriculum materials they choose in order to be effective. They are the principles or propositions that undergird and guide teachers' appreciations, decisions, and actions.* (54–55)

Practical theories held by the teachers provide the "reasons why teachers do what they do" (56), and the actions taken by the teacher are the manifestations of these theories. The source of the theories is eclectic, drawing on research-based information, experience, and the particulars of the circumstances in which the theories are employed.

When engaging in a process of change with teachers, whether it be about new curriculum, new instructional strategies, or assessment practices, it is important to understand who the teacher is and what his or her priorities and assumptions are. This approach to professional development places emphasis on existing mind-sets in addition to introducing new ideas, strategies, or skills. Thus, a *personal approach* to working with teachers on assessment-related issues promotes the examination and articulation of the teacher's current assessment practices and considers how the teacher can be actively engaged in deciding how to make innovations in his or her own classroom.

An Illustration

The Classroom Assessment Project to Improve Teaching and Learning (CAPITAL), a National Science Foundation[1]–funded project, was conducted by Stanford University in partnership with five school districts in the San Francisco Bay Region from 1998 through 2003. The project worked with teachers in a close collaboration to examine classroom assessment practices in middle school science. The science teachers who worked in the project shared a desire to improve their classroom assessment practices and engaged in a form of collaborative action research—identifying aspects of their everyday assessment practices that they explored through a process of inquiry, with the intention of making changes in their classrooms.

The CAPITAL staff approached their work with teachers from the perspective that teachers' practical theories, their beliefs about assessment, about students, and about themselves influenced their instructional practices and would also help determine the changes they chose to make in those practices. Project staff met regularly with the participating teachers individually and in small groups to discuss classroom innovations, to address struggles the teachers were facing, and to raise questions about assessment practices. In these discussions, the teachers reflected on their teaching practices and the modifications they were making in instruction and assessment. When appropriate, university staff offered suggestions and ideas about assessment. Generally, the university staff served as facilitators of discussion, raising questions that would elicit more elaborate descriptions and reasoning behind decisions made by the teachers.

CAPITAL staff did not begin their work with teachers with preconceived ideas about desired changes in classroom practice. Rather, they focused on the teachers' emerging interests and priorities. The nature of the interaction with each teacher and each group of teachers varied, depending on who the teachers were and what they identified as their needs. The project team played different roles with the individual teachers: a mirror reflecting back to the teacher aspects of his or her teaching; a second pair of eyes or ears in the classroom to document classroom interactions; a

---

[1] National Science Foundation Grant REC-9909370

videographer who captured classroom interactions for future reflection and analysis; a critical friend who raised questions for further consideration.

Relationships with teachers took time to develop and cultivate. The joint work between university staff and classroom teachers was intense, drawing on each member of the project both professionally and personally. Delving into questions about the goals that the teacher had for his or her students, why the teacher made particular choices in the classroom, or how information would be used required that the teachers trust the university staff and that the university staff trust the teachers. This approach to working with teachers was personal (Coffey, Sato, and Schneider 2001). It was work that took place in their classrooms, examined the issues that they deemed important, and investigated the ways that their personal views about teaching and learning influenced their teaching.

Through this focused approach with small groups and individual teachers, CAPITAL staff and teachers came to understand how important teachers' beliefs are in their carrying out of assessment. The following examples from the project illustrate this point.

One teacher participating in the project began teaching as a second career after working for decades in a biology laboratory. This piece of biographical information is important for understanding how this teacher views everyday assessment. Assessment is firmly grounded in evidence from her classroom. She carefully examines student work and maintains detailed records of what the students have completed. Much like a scientist drawing upon empirical evidence when making inferences or drawing conclusions, this teacher regularly uses her data to make judgments about students' progress. This is also the case in her everyday interactions in the classroom. She listens to students while they work independently and in groups to learn about what they are thinking, and she weighs what she learns from her observations with what she expects before moving forward with instruction.

This teacher's work within CAPITAL centered on the examination of how students understand particular concepts about the practice of science. This focus again stemmed from the teacher's deep interest—one might call it a *passion*—in science as an enterprise practiced by people. Particularly, she was interested in the students' skills and understanding about data analysis. She designed her science curriculum so as to return to questions of data analysis iteratively throughout the school year. She raised questions such as how to support the learning of the idea of error in scientific measurements through scientific investigation and subsequent data analysis; how to help students understand the concept of "average" and its relationship to multiple trials of a scientific investigation; and how to help students understand the accuracy of scientific instrumentation and the limitations that the instrumentation places on scientific investigations.

This teacher's work in investigating assessment practices in her classroom arose from her own interests in science as a discipline comprising not solely factual information, but also concepts of accepted practice and procedure for scientific investigation and analysis. Her interests led her to link her explorations of her assessment practices tightly to the scientific practices that she valued from her own experience as a scientist. This pursuit was not trivial. She plumbed the depths of scientific concepts and identified nuances in student understanding of these concepts through her analysis of student work and her careful listening in the classroom. In this case, both the methods of investigating assessment practices and the substance of the investigations related to the teacher's personal experience and who she is as a person.

Another teacher entered teaching as a career because he was determined to try to make school a positive and productive experience for students who have traditionally been marginalized by the system. For this teacher, social justice and equitable opportunities for students were foundational to his work as a teacher and what he believed in deeply as a person. One of his goals in his work with CAPITAL was to "find lots of possible ways for kids to be successful." When he first began working with CAPITAL, he viewed traditional assessment practices as processes that had damaged students' self-esteem, that had treated students unfairly, and that were designed to punish students. He was very interested in figuring out how assessment in his classroom could support students in their endeavors to learn science and how assessment could encourage students to engage in his science class, rather than discouraging them from doing so.

One of the strategies that this teacher implemented was to allow students to work on assignments until the assignments met the teacher's standards. Students could get written or verbal feedback from the teacher and continue to improve their work until it received an A. Knowing that they could correct, revise, or polish their work helped the students view their efforts as a process for engaging in learning rather than as a process of production. Students who had not been successful in traditional grading systems were now able to engage in the work without fear of imminent failure.

For this teacher, everyday assessment was not merely about assigning grades. He saw assessment as a means to encourage participation in science and to nurture success. In his view, if the students eventually demonstrated that they understood a concept or could perform a skill, it did not matter how many times they had to revise their work. To implement this assessment technique, the teacher had to develop strategies of giving meaningful feedback that the students could act on. He struggled with the amount of time that it took to provide multiple rounds of feedback. However, the payoff of greater student involvement and higher quality work were meaningful to him and his beliefs about what his students needed to be successful.

A Collaborative Personal Approach

CAPITAL was founded on the principle that teachers' understanding about their own teaching is deepened when they discuss their experiences with peers who are trying to make similar changes (Atkin 1994; Wineburg and Grossman 1998). Not only do the teachers learn more about their practice, but they also develop a heightened awareness of their sense of self-as-teacher while engaged in communities of like-minded colleagues (Lave and Wegner 1991). Teachers who work in CAPITAL devise what they want to explore with regard to assessment. They try innovations in their classrooms and periodically come together to talk about what they have done and what they have learned from their forays into assessment in their everyday practices. Again, an illustration from the project will demonstrate this principle in action.

A group of teachers from the same school district recently reflected together on their work in CAPITAL. One of the teachers recounted how an expert in the development of rubrics for assessing student performance had given a presentation at her school. She said that she found the presentation interesting and she could see how she might use some of the ideas, but she did not have the opportunity to try them out and explore how the rubrics might work in her classroom. Further, she emphasized the value of having time within CAPITAL to convene with her colleagues and discuss the strategies and innovations she has since tried in her classroom.

This consultation and deliberation time gave this group of five teachers time to reflect on their assessment practices, garner new ideas and refinements from other experienced teachers, and make connections to broader and deeper issues related to assessment. For example, this group of teachers began their work on everyday assessment with CAPITAL with a desire to reduce the amount of paperwork they were handling in the process of collecting and grading daily assignments from the more than 150 students they saw each day. They were feeling overwhelmed and wanted to work on ways to streamline their grading practices. At first blush, this pursuit might have seemed self-serving, as one of the teachers described it after a year of working with the project. Through the discussions about strategies to reduce all the paperwork, however, the teachers began to raise questions about what it was that they were fundamentally assessing about their students by collecting homework and classwork every day. Together, they came to a realization that much of their time was spent keeping records of completion of assignments without a clear focus on whether or what the students were learning. The backlog of paper that accumulated sometimes meant that students did not get their assignments back for weeks. Jointly, the teachers realized that the comments they made on student work may not have the desired impact, given that the assignment was weeks old when it was returned; furthermore, students felt no responsibility for reading or responding to the comments the teacher had painstakingly made on their completed work. The teachers began to explore ideas about the importance of timely feedback, whether verbal or written, *while* the students were engaged with the assignment.

As a result of these discussions, the teachers began to look more closely at the actual assignments they were asking the students to complete. Their desire for greater efficiency in their grading led them to ask themselves why they assigned particular projects and what they thought students would learn from the assignment and to develop strategies that would allow them to give feedback to students *while* the students were working on their assignments. The teachers had begun the discussion with an understanding of assessment as a process of keeping track of students' completed work. Through their classroom inquiries, deliberations with colleagues pursuing similar lines of investigation, and the periodic input from the university staff, the teachers began to see assessment as a process to support learning in a timely and ongoing fashion. Their collaboration prompted deeper thinking about their assessment practices and led to a variety of practical, innovative projects with clear learning goals and to new processes of giving feedback to students.

One of the teachers described how the process of discussion is critical to understanding how new techniques can best be implemented in the classroom: "When we try to explain what we have done to other teachers, they get excited about our ideas. But when they don't have the opportunity to discuss it after they have tried it out, they don't get it." This insight speaks to the importance of not only introducing new ideas to teachers, but also allowing for opportunities to reflect with others on how to tailor these ideas to meet the needs of particular teachers.

Implications for Working with Teachers

How does this personal approach to working with teachers fit into a broader view of professional development? In recent years, the professional development community has reached consensus about principles for the design of high-quality professional development for teachers (Hawley and Valli 1999, 139–44):

Principle one: Professional development should be driven by analyses of the differences between goals and standards for student learning and student performance.

Principle two: Professional development should involve learners (such as teachers) in the identification of what they need to learn and, when possible, in the development of the learning opportunity and the process to be used.

Principle three: Professional development should be primarily school based and integral to school operations.

Principle four: Professional development should provide learning opportunities that relate to individual needs but for the most part are organized around collaborative problem solving.

Principle five: Professional development should be continuous and ongoing, involving follow-up and support for further learning, including support from sources external to the school that can provide necessary resources and an outside perspective.

Principle six: Professional development should incorporate evaluation of multiple sources of information on outcomes for students and processes that are involved in implementing the lessons learned through professional development.

Principle seven: *Professional development should provide opportunities to engage in developing a theoretical understanding of the knowledge and skills to be learned.*

Principle eight: *Professional development should be integrated with a comprehensive change process that deals with impediments to facilitators of student learning.*

The personal approach to working with teachers described in this chapter is not in conflict with any of these principles, and the CAPITAL example demonstrates how principles two, three, four, five, and seven can be put into action. With appropriate attention to the role that the teacher plays in the design of professional development, principles one, six, and eight can also be addressed while maintaining a focus on individual teachers' classrooms and personal changes.

I am not suggesting that a personal approach is appropriate for all teachers or all programs. An individualized and personal approach to professional development is time, personnel, and resource demanding. Large-scale reform efforts that are focused on instructional change are usually economically constrained and thus seek efficient methods by which to introduce teachers to reform ideas and practices. Professional development models that emphasize the dissemination of information to teachers or those that seek to train teachers in particular pedagogical skills typically do not pay attention to the individual teacher's interpretation of the information and skills into his or her practice. As Mrs. Oublier respectfully demonstrated, the translation to practice does not always carry with it the spirit of the intended change. If complex change is expected, then alternative models of professional development must engage teachers in ongoing examination of practice, rethink how teachers' time is spent in schools, provide structural and cultural support for teachers to engage in new practices, and value teacher change as not just a process of implementing new behaviors but also as a process of personal change.

Summary and Conclusion

Everyday assessment is embedded in the ongoing interactions in the classroom. For example, teachers make instructional decisions based on how a student responds to a question posed during class discussion, students reflect on their own confidence in understanding a concept, and students judge the quality of their own work and the work of their peers. Professional development aimed specifically at everyday classroom assessment, then, must approach the realm of assessment with a broader view of when assessment occurs and how information is used in the classroom. While it is important for teachers to learn how to design appropriate stand-alone assessments, professional development aimed at everyday assessment must focus more broadly on the teaching and learning interactions and address how the teacher's approach to assessment fits into his or her overall instructional practice.

In this chapter, I have discussed how work with teachers in assessment-related professional development can be approached from a personal perspective. While introducing new ideas, strategies, techniques, and skills to teachers is an important aspect of professional learning, this is only part of the process for working with teachers to bring about new understanding or change in their classrooms. What a teacher knows and can do is only a partial determinant of how he or she acts in the classroom. A teacher's actions are also shaped by his or her contexts, beliefs, values, and prior experiences. Teachers are often driven to action by their enthusiasm and their passions. Professional development that helps teachers to identify and articulate their needs, interests, and passions taps into the teacher's individual desires. A personal approach to working with teachers values what the individual teacher brings to the professional development experience, recognizes that the teacher's beliefs and prior experiences will have great influence on how new practices and innovations are enacted in the classroom, and allows the teacher to determine his or her priorities for change.

References

Atkin, J. M. 1994. Teacher research to change policy. In *Teacher research and educational reform: 93rd yearbook of the National Society for the Study of Education*, Part I, eds. S. Hollingsworth and H. Sockett. Chicago: University of Chicago Press.

Atkin, J. M., P. Black, and J. Coffey, eds. 2001. *Classroom assessment and the national science education standards.* Washington, DC: National Academy Press.

Coffey, J., M. Sato, and B. Schneider. 2001. *Classroom assessment—Up close and personal.* Paper presented at the annual meeting of the American Educational Research Association, Seattle, WA (April).

Cohen, D. K. 1990. A revolution in one classroom: The case of Mrs. Oublier. *Educational Evaluation and Policy Analysis* 12(3): 311–29.

Hawley, W. D., and L. Valli. 1999. The essentials of effective professional development: A new consensus. In *Teaching as the learning profession: Handbook for policy and practice*, eds. L. Darling-Hammond and G. Sykes. San Francisco: Jossey-Bass.

Lave, J., and E. Wegner. 1991. *Situated learning: Legitimate peripheral participation.* Cambridge: Cambridge University Press.

Sadler, R. 1989. Formative assessment and the design of instructional systems. *Instructional Science* 18: 119–44.

Sanders, D. and G. McCutcheon. 1986. The development of practical theories of teaching. *Journal of Curriculum and Supervision* 2: 50–67.

Stiggins, R. J. 2002. Assessment crisis: The absence of assessment FOR learning. *Phi Delta Kappan* 83(10).

Wenger, E. 1998. *Communities of practice.* Cambridge: Cambridge University Press.

Wineburg, S., and P. Grossman. 1998. Creating a community of learners among high school teachers. *Phi Delta Kappan* 79(5): 350–53.

Reconsidering Large-Scale Assessment to Heighten Its Relevance to Learning

Lorrie A. Shepard

Lorrie Shepard is dean of the School of Education at the University of Colorado at Boulder. She has served as president of the American Educational Research Association, president of the National Council on Measurement in Education, and vice president of the National Academy of Education. Her research focuses on psychometrics and the use and misuse of tests in educational settings. Specific studies address standard setting, the influence of tests on instruction, teacher testing, identification of mild handicaps, and early childhood assessment. Currently, her work focuses on the use of classroom assessment to support teaching and learning.

Many science teachers have been affected indirectly by high-stakes, account-ability pressures as they watch attention and resources flow to language arts and mathematics instruction—because these subjects are tested. Others have experienced firsthand the ways that external science assessments can undermine inquiry-based curricula and efforts to teach for understanding. Is it possible to counteract these effects and make external, large-scale assessments more relevant to student learning? How can large-scale assessments, remote from the classroom, serve instructional purposes?

I agreed to write a chapter addressing these questions with some trepidation because the history of assessment reform has not been pretty. Ideally, evaluation data should be used to improve instructional programs and thus ensure meaningful learning opportunities for students. The difficulty with promoting an ideal, however, is that we have all seen how a lofty goal can be corrupted when pursued on the cheap or when too many participants hold conflicting ideas about what was intended. A decade ago, standards-based reformers, recognizing the deleterious effects of traditional, multiple-choice tests on ambitious learning goals, promised to create "authentic assessments" and "tests worth teaching to." These promises have not been realized, however, in part because accountability advocates have pursued the slogan of high standards without necessarily subscribing to the underlying theory calling for profound changes in curriculum, instruction, and assessment.

The central aim of this chapter is to consider how large-scale assessments could be redesigned to heighten their contribution to student learning. In this section, which acts as a preamble, I (1) explain why assessments must be designed and validated differently for different purposes and the implications of this differentiation for large-scale assessments and (2) summarize the essential features of effective classroom assessment. While classroom assessment is not the focus of this chapter, we cannot consider here how large-scale assessment could be made compatible with and supportive of classroom instruction and assessment without a shared understanding of effective classroom assessment. In the next, main section of the chapter I address the important purposes served by large-scale assessment: (1) exemplification of learning goals, (2) program "diagnosis," and (3) certification or "screening" of individual student achievement. In addition, large-scale assessments can serve as a site or impetus for professional development to enhance the use of learning-centered classroom assessment. I conclude with an analysis of the impediments to change and recommendations for addressing these challenges.

Assessments Designed for Different Purposes

To the layperson, a test is a test. So why couldn't the same test be used to diagnose student learning needs; to judge the effectiveness of teachers, schools, districts, and states; and to compare U.S. schools to the schools of other nations? For measurement specialists, however, purpose matters. Purpose shapes test design and alters the criteria for evaluating the reliability and validity of the test. According to the *Standards for Educational and Psychological Testing* (AERA, APA, NCME 1999), "No test will serve all purposes equally well. Choices in test development and evaluation that enhance validity for one purpose may diminish validity for other purposes" (145).

Large-scale assessments are used to monitor achievement trends over time and to hold schools and school districts accountable. In some states, large-scale assessments are also used to make high-stakes decisions about individual teachers and students—for example, in regard to teacher pay increases, grade-to-grade promotion, or graduation from high school. Because of the significant consequences that follow from the results, large-scale assessments must be highly reliable. Thus, purpose shapes technical requirements. And, to be fair, large-scale assessment data must be collected in a standardized way to ensure comparability across schools. It would be unfair, for example, if one school gave the test a month later than other schools, explained unfamiliar words to students, or allowed extra time when students hadn't finished.[1] Because of the cost of ensuring reliability and standardization and because of the intrusion on instructional time, large-scale assessments are administered only once per year and must necessarily be broad, "survey" instruments touching lightly on the many curricular topics and skills taught throughout the year.

In contrast, classroom assessments intended to help students learn must be closely tied to particular units of instruction and must be used in the particular days and weeks when students are learning specific concepts. To be truly diagnostic, teacher's questions must probe students' understandings and push to identify extensions where mastery is incomplete or where misconceptions impede learning. Because formative assessment in classrooms is intended to help target the next instructional steps, not to assign official proficiency status, there is much less need for formal assessment procedures or adherence to strict reliability standards. Mismeasurement of a student's knowledge and skills by a teacher one day can be overturned by subsequent assessments in the next day or week.

---

[1] Note that sources of unfairness to students caused by differences in students' experiences with and opportunities to learn tested content are not corrected by standardization.

Knowing What Students Know (Pellegrino, Chudowsky, and Glaser 2001) is a landmark report published recently by the National Academy of Sciences that brings together the knowledge bases of cognitive learning theory and measurement science. Its authors similarly address this link between purpose and assessment requirements, referring to the inevitability of *trade-offs* in assessment design: "Ironically, the questions that are of most use to the state officer are of the least use to the teacher" (224). One way to help policy makers understand the limitations of an external, once-per-year test for instructional purposes is to point out that good teachers should already know so much about their students that they could fill out the test booklet for them. "I'm sure Maria can do problems 1, 3, and 4. But she will struggle with problems 2 and 5 because she hasn't mastered those skills yet." To be effective in supporting learning, teachers need in-depth assessments targeted to the gray areas where they don't know what their students are thinking.

The following distinctions highlight the differences between large-scale and classroom-level assessments, which imply that notably different assessment strategies are needed.

- Standardized vs. dynamic

- Uniform date vs. ongoing dates

- Independent performance vs. assisted performance

- Delayed feedback vs. immediate feedback

- Stringent requirements for technical accuracy vs. less stringent requirements

For example, it is appropriate to provide hints or to alter the task while assessing for classroom purposes because in so doing the teacher learns what a student can do independently and pinpoints precisely where understanding breaks down.

In contrast to these distinctions, the single most important shared characteristic of large-scale and classroom assessments should be their *alignment* with curriculum standards. Here I do not mean the limited alignment obtained when test publishers show that all of their multiple-choice items can be matched to the categories of a state's content standards. Rather, I am speaking of the more complete and substantive alignment that occurs when the tasks, problems, and projects in which students are engaged represent the range and depth of what we say we want students to understand and be able to do. Perhaps a better word would be *embodiment*. Assessments at either level should embody and fully represent important learning goals. In science, we can use the National Science Education Standards (NRC 1996) as our learning targets. Assessments at both the large-scale and classroom levels, then, must embody the fundamental concepts, principles, and inquiry skills needed to conduct investigations and evaluate scientific findings as identified by the standards.

For large-scale and classroom assessments to be symbiotic, they must share this common understanding of what it means to do good work in a discipline and ideally hold a common view of how that expertise develops over time (Pellegrino, Chudowsky, and Glaser 2001). When the conception of curriculum represented by a state's large-scale assessment is at odds with content standards and curricular goals, then the ill effects of teaching to the external, high-stakes test, especially curriculum distortion and nongeneralizable test score gains, will be exaggerated, and it will be more difficult for teachers to use classroom assessment strategies that support conceptual understanding while at the same time working to improve student performance on the state test.

A Model of Classroom Assessment in Support of Learning

Classroom assessment is both formal—involving quizzes, exams, laboratory assignments, and projects—and informal—involving journal entries, observations, and oral questioning. It also serves both formative and summative purposes, depending on whether assessment insights are used to help students take the next steps in learning or to report on the level of achievement attained to date. A rich research literature shows us the dramatic achievement gains that can occur when formative assessment is used (Black and Wiliam 1998; Shepard 2000). Most surveys of practice, however, find that assessment is more often used for grading than for learning.

An ideal model of classroom assessment must address both content and process considerations. The activities in which students engage and the work we ask them to produce determine the real targets of learning regardless of what goals might be stated in curriculum guidelines or lesson plans. Therefore, it is essential that the content of instructional activities capture the big ideas and inquiry skills of the National Science Education Standards. Formative assessments are then embedded within these instructional activities. A student's ability to communicate scientific information might be assessed, for example, when presenting a group's findings to the rest of the class. As implementation of standards-based reform progresses, a bigger challenge is to ensure that summative classroom measures also mirror the standards. Too often, classroom tests measure what is easiest to measure—vocabulary definitions and restatement of laws and principles—rather than, say, the ability to use principles and laws to make a prediction or explain a result. As suggested in the science standards document, improving the content of assessment means "assessing what is most highly valued, assessing rich, well-structured knowledge, and assessing scientific understanding and reasoning" (NRC 1996, 100). Effective classroom assessment also departs from traditional practice in the way assessment is used, becoming much more interactive and a part of the learning process. As documented in research studies (Black and Wiliam 1998; Pellegrino, Chudowsky, and Glaser 2001; Shepard 2000), effective assessment

- activates and builds on prior knowledge,

- makes students' thinking visible and explicit,

- engages students in self-monitoring of their own learning,

- makes the features of good work understandable and accessible to students, and

- provides feedback specifically targeted toward improvement.

These elements can be made a part of everyday instructional routines, using a definition of formative assessment developed by Sadler (1989) and another recent National Research Council report, *Classroom Assessment and the National Science Education Standards* (Atkin, Black, and Coffey 2001). For assessment to be *formative* in the sense of moving learning forward, three questions are asked: (1) Where are you trying to go? (2) Where are you now? (3) How can you get there? It is because of the explicitness of these steps and the focused effort to close the gap between 1 and 2 that assessment actually contributes to learning. Elsewhere I have also argued that effective use of these strategies requires a cultural shift in classrooms so that students are less concerned about grades and hiding what they don't know and are more focused on using feedback and support from teachers and classmates to learn—that is, to solve a problem, improve a piece of writing, or figure out *why* an answer is correct.

Finally, to be effective, classroom assessment will need to find ways to address the many negative effects of grading on student motivation. Cognitive studies have shown us that making criteria explicit will improve student-learning outcomes (Fredericksen and Collins 1989). But motivational psychologists have found that traditional grading practices may negatively affect students' intrinsic motivation, their sense of self-efficacy, and their willingness to expend effort or tackle difficult problems. Therefore, merely sharing grading criteria will not automatically eliminate the negative effects of grading.

Unlike the extensive amount of work on formative assessment in recent years, there has been much less attention, outside of the motivational literature, to the type of grading policies that would improve rather than decrease motivation. Self-assessment is one example of a change in classroom practice that could serve both cognitive and motivational ends. Self-assessment makes the features of excellent work explicit and helps students internalize these criteria (thus serving cognitive purposes). At the same time, asking students to self-assess according to well-defined criteria establishes a mastery rather than normative definition of success, conveys developing competence, and illustrates how effort could lead to improvement, all of which enhance motivation (Stipek 1996). More work needs to be done to relate formative and summative assessment within classrooms. Perhaps all formative assessment should be reserved exclusively for learning purposes, not for grading—even while eventual summative criteria are used formatively. Note that pursuit of this idea would run against the highly litigious point systems that many teachers currently use to track every assignment and to justify grades.

Purposes Served By Large-Scale Assessment

Large-scale assessments such as the Third International Math and Science Survey (TIMSS), the National Assessment of Education Progress (NAEP), and various state- and district-level assessment programs are used to measure student achievement for aggregate units (nations, states, districts, schools), to track changes in achievement for these units over time, and sometimes to measure the performance of individual students. If the content of a large-scale assessment adequately represents ambitious curricular goals—as called for in the science standards, for example—then large-scale assessment can become an integral part of curricular reform and instructional improvement efforts. Such an assessment program could be used to: exemplify important learning goals; diagnose program strengths and weaknesses; report on the proficiency status of individual students; and, through associated professional development opportunities, improve teachers' abilities to teach to the standards and at the same time become more adept in using formative assessment. These purposes would not be served, however, by traditional, multiple-choice-only tests that do not adequately embody the National Science Education Standards.

Exemplification of Learning Goals

The science standards developed a vision for science instruction by drawing on best practices, but for many teachers the standards call for significant changes in practice—away from vocabulary-laden textbooks and toward more inquiry-based approaches. For many, these hoped-for changes may seem out of reach either conceptually or practically. Large-scale assessments can give life to the standards expectations by illustrating the kinds of skills and conceptual understandings that students are expected to have mastered. Moreover, because some of the very best assessment tasks would also qualify as good instructional activities, released assessment items can help to raise awareness about the kinds of instructional opportunities students need if they are to develop deep understandings and effective inquiry skills.

The performance task illustrated in Figure 1 is taken from *A Sampler of Science Assessment* developed by Kathy Comfort and others in the California Department of Education (1994). The task gives eighth-grade students hands-on experience with subduction and asks them to generalize their understandings from the physical model to information about California landmarks. One could reasonably expect that students who had had previous instruction on geological processes and plate tectonics would do well on this task. If, however, students with textbook exposure to these ideas faltered in providing explanations, the assessment experience might prompt teachers to consider using more conceptual learning tools in the future, and, in fact, the investigation shown in Figure 1 is an example of the type of instructional activity needed.

Figure 1. Grade-Eight Performance Task Illustrating Hands-On Instruction and Assessment Focused on "Big Ideas"

**Grade Eight Performance Task
Student Instructions for *The Fault Line***

> Standing near the railroad track waiting for help to arrive, Joe looked around at the mountains, their rocks all twisted and folded. He'd been on this track for ten years and had never noticed the rocks before! How do they get like that, he wondered.

Directions:

In this investigation you will examine the process that causes rock layers to fold and twist.

Part A

■ Follow the directions to set up your plate model.

Set up your plate model as shown in this picture.

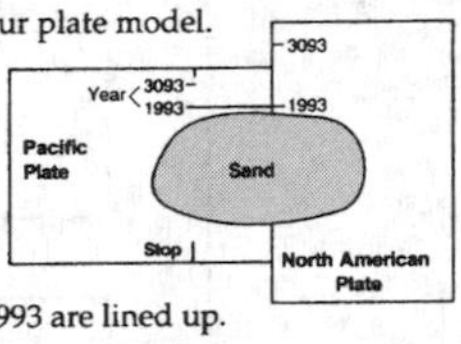

1. Check that the lines marked 1993 are lined up.
2. Place about 100 ml of sand on your plate models as in the picture above.
3. Smooth the sand into a thin layer.
4. Slowly slide the Pacific Plate along the 1993 line until "Stop" is even with the edge of the North American Plate.

Slowly slide the Pacific Plate along the 1993 line until "Stop" is even with the edge of the North American Plate.

— Slide ➔

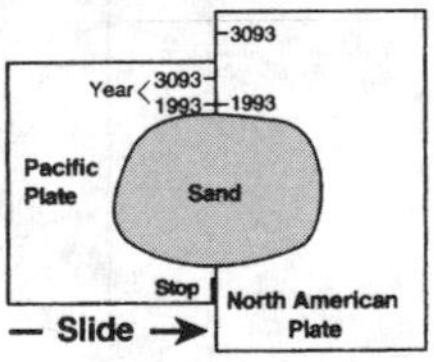

■ Do not move your plate model. Go on to answer the questions on the next page.

Grade Eight Performance Task Questions for *The Fault Line* – Components 1 and 2

COMPONENT 1

■ After you have worked with the plate model, answer the following questions completely.

1. Describe what happened to the sand when you slid one plate beneath the other.

COMPONENT 2

2. Would the direction of the plate movement affect the formation of the mountains? Explain how.

(Continues on next page.)

Source: Reprinted, by permission, from *A sampler of science assessment*, copyright 1994, California Department of Education, P.O. Box 271, Sacramento, CA 95812-0271.

(Figure 1. continued)

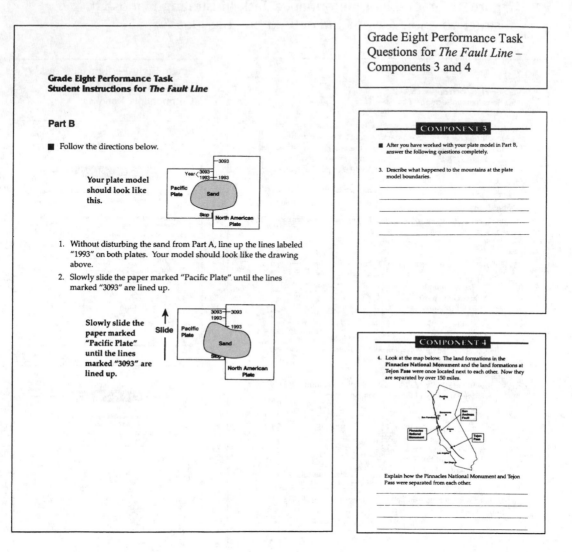

Grade Eight Performance Task Student Instructions for *The Fault Line*

Part B

■ Follow the directions below.

Your plate model should look like this.

1. Without disturbing the sand from Part A, line up the lines labeled "1993" on both plates. Your model should look like the drawing above.

2. Slowly slide the paper marked "Pacific Plate" until the lines marked "3093" are lined up.

Slowly slide the paper marked "Pacific Plate" until the lines marked "3093" are lined up.

Grade Eight Performance Task Questions for *The Fault Line* – Components 3 and 4

COMPONENT 3

■ After you have worked with your plate model in Part B, answer the following questions completely.

3. Describe what happened to the mountains at the plate model boundaries.

COMPONENT 4

4. Look at the map below. The land formations in the Pinnacles National Monument and the land formations at Tejon Pass were once located next to each other. Now they are separated by over 150 miles.

Explain how the Pinnacles National Monument and Tejon Pass were separated from each other.

In some cases a single conceptual question, if used reflectively, can prompt teachers to reconsider the efficacy of their instructional approach. In some sense, Phil Sadler's classic films, *A Private Universe* and *Minds of Our Own* are each based on one significant conceptual question. Can you explain what makes the seasons? Can you use a wire, a bulb, and a battery and make the bulb light? The fact that so many Harvard graduates struggled with the first question, and MIT graduates with the second, has prompted many science teachers to think again about what their students are really understanding when they pass traditional tests. Thus, if a state assessment reflects the National Science Education Standards it serves both as a model of what's expected for student mastery and also of the kinds of instructional activities that would enable that mastery.

In preparing to write this chapter, I asked experts in several states to comment on my outline of large-scale assessment purposes and to provide examples of each application where appropriate. Rachel Wood, Education Associate in Science, and Julie Schmidt, Director of Science, are part of the science leadership team responsible for the development of Delaware's Comprehensive Assessment Program. They responded with a detailed commentary, recounting their experiences in involving science teachers in development of summative assessments for curriculum modules (as part of the National Science Foundation's Local Systemic Change Initiative) concurrent with development of the state's on-demand test. Here's what they said about the role of assessment in leading instructional change.

What was not appreciated early on is that assessment would become the driver for realizing what it meant to "meet the standards." Initially assessment was seen more as an appendage to curriculum. That was due, in part, to the early recall nature of assessments that contributed minimally in diagnosing student learning, whereas curriculum laid out a road map to follow. Later (after the assessments changed dramatically), it was clearer that assessment indicated whether you reached your destination or not. In other words, the task of the leadership and its team was building a consensus around quality student work in science. This consensus had to be founded upon a different model of student learning than the model most teachers possessed. (Wood and Schmidt 2002)

Program "Diagnosis"

It is popular these days to talk about making large-scale assessments more diagnostic. Colorado's Governor Bill Owens has said that he wants "to turn the annual CSAP exam from just a snapshot of student performance into a diagnostic tool to bring up a child's math, reading, and writing scores" (Whaley 2002). And in the No Child Left Behind Act of 2001, state plans are required to include assessments that "produce individual student interpretive, descriptive, and diagnostic reports, ... that allow parents, teachers, and principals to understand and address the specific academic needs of students." In the next subsection, on individual student "screening," I explain what kinds of information a once-per-year test could reasonably provide on individual students' learning. We should be clear that large-scale assessments cannot be diagnostic of *individual* learning needs in the same way that classroom assessments can be. What large-scale assessments can do is "diagnose" *program* strengths and weaknesses. Typically we refer to this as the program evaluation purpose of large-scale assessment.

When content frameworks used in test construction have sufficient numbers of items by content and processes strands, then it is possible to report assessment results by meaningful subscores. For example, it would be possible for a school to know whether its students were doing relatively better (compared to state normative data) on declarative knowledge items or on problems requiring conceptual understanding. It is also possible to report on relative strengths and weaknesses according to content categories: life science, physical science, Earth and space science, science and technology, and science in personal and social perspectives. This type of profile analysis would let a school or district know whether its performance in technology was falling behind performance in other areas, or whether there were significant gender effects by content category. For example, we might anticipate that girls would do better in science programs that emphasize the relevance of science to personal and social perspectives, while boys might do relatively better in applications of technology. Results such as these might prompt important instructional conversations about how to teach to strengths while not presuming that either group was incapable of mastering material in their traditional area of weakness.

In addition to subtest profiles, particular assessment items can sometimes yield important program diagnostic information. Wood and Schmidt (2002) provide the following examples of conceptual errors and skill weaknesses revealed by assessment results that warranted attention in subsequent professional development efforts.

For instance, an eighth-grade weather assessment revealed that students across the state have over-generalized their knowledge of the movement of all air masses as having to go from west to east. In the classroom, students are studying the movement of weather fronts and predicting weather patterns, many of which do move from west to east. That piece of understanding has now been applied to the movement of all air masses. They are unable to explain ocean breezes on the east coast with this model or Bermuda highs that they experience in their daily lives. This information was not uncovered through a question about weather patterns in the United States but by using a question on land and sea breezes. There is now an opportunity to address this issue in professional development because this suggests that the idea originates from some connection made in the classroom. This confirms what we mentioned earlier, that students are indeed constructing knowledge in the classroom that teachers might not be aware of unless they search for it. Most teachers are probably delighted that students have the idea that most weather fronts move from west to east, but were unaware that students would over-generalize, unless the class has an opportunity to work through the limits of a "rule" or model.

And a second example:

Analysis of item statistics from the state test reveals major weaknesses that the leadership can address through professional development. For example, questions asking students to construct or interpret a simple graph indicate that students were not being given enough opportunities to graph data and analyze the results, compare graphs, or draw conclusions from the kind of graph that might appear in the newspaper, etc.... One item, for example, with a P-value of .31 in simple graphing indicated an alarming weakness. A P-value of .80 was expected. As a result the leadership selected graphing items, rubrics, and samples of student responses with P-values to focus discussion on the instructional implications of the student responses.... Some of the lead teachers participated in the piloting of released items and were stunned that their own students were performing at a level that confirmed the P-value found for the whole state.

Because large-scale assessments are broad survey instruments, test makers often have difficulty providing very detailed feedback for curriculum evaluation beyond major subtest categories. This is especially true for assessments like TIMSS and NAEP that cross many jurisdictions and may also be true for state assessments when each district has its own curriculum. Cross-jurisdictional assessments invariably become more generic in how they assess achievement, using questions that call for reasoning with basic content (like on the ACT) rather than presenting the type of question that would be appropriate in a specific course examination. The need for items to be accessible to all students, regardless of what particular science curriculum they have followed, explains why so many NAEP items, for example, involve reading data from a table or graph to draw an inference or support a conclusion, because such items are self-contained and do not presume particular content knowledge. Unfortunately, generic, reasoning items are not very diagnostic nor do they further the goal of exemplifying standards.

How then could we have more instructionally relevant items, like the earlier California example? If state assessment frameworks were to stipulate specific in-depth problem types they intended to use, there would a danger that teachers would teach to the specific item types instead of the larger domain. Conversely, if different in-depth problems were used each year representing the full domain, teachers would be likely to complain about the unpredictability and unfairness of the assessment. Again, I quote extensively from commentary by Wood and Schmidt (2002). They have documented the power of released items (accompanied by student papers and scoring guides) both to exemplify standards and to diagnose gaps in students' learning. Here's how they wrestled with the dilemma of fostering teaching to standards without encouraging teaching to the test.

Many classroom teachers who haven't had the opportunity to be directly engaged in the lead teacher program hold a different view of the test and items than those involved in the assessment development. For instance, classroom teachers express frustration at the comprehensive nature of the standards and not being able to determine "what items" are going to be on the next test. They complain that we don't release entire forms each year for their students to practice in the classroom in preparation for the next year's test. What has been released and is preferable to release are not isolated items matched to a standard, but an insightful commentary about how and where the concepts in the released items fit into a larger sequence of student conceptual understanding. Teachers will revert back to second-guessing the test items if presented a released item decontextualized from an analysis that helps explain how and why students are struggling with the concept that the item is measuring. For example, when many high school students were unable to construct a simple monohybrid Punnett square and determine the genotypes of both parents and offspring, teachers could easily have thought, "I taught them that, they should know it" or "I guess I need to teach more Punnett squares"—which suggests that it is being taught in a mechanical approach. But the commentary around the released item attempts to turn teachers' attention toward thinking about how students have acquired only a mechanical sense and don't understand why you would have a Punnett square in the first place.

The example in Figure 2 shows how the analysis accompanying the released item is intended to focus attention on underlying concepts that students might not be understanding. "This particular item taps both procedural and conceptual knowledge, while most teachers think it is only procedural knowledge" (Wood and Schmidt 2002). Because teachers focus on procedural knowledge, students assume the Punnett square is an end in itself rather than a tool for reasoning through possible gene combinations. Lacking conceptual knowledge, they are likely to stack up illogical numbers of alleles in each cell. Wood and Schmidt's analysis is intended to try and reconnect the specific test question to a larger instructional domain, which should be the appropriate target of improvement efforts.

Certification or "Screening" of Individual Student Achievement

Historically, many state assessment programs were designed to imitate the NAEP; they provided broad content coverage and were used primarily for program evaluation. NAEP does not produce individual student scores. In fact, using the strategy of matrix sampling, each participating student takes only a small fraction of the items in the total test pool so as to minimize testing time and ensure a rich representation of the content domain. In recent years, under pressure to provide more accountability information, many assessment programs have abandoned their matrix sampling designs and instead give the same test to every student so that individual scores can be reported. The No Child Left Behind Act requires all states to produce student scores in reading and mathematics in grades three to eight, with testing in science in certain grades to begin in 2007–2008. Individual reporting of students' proficiency status is a type of certification testing, not unlike a licensure test—with accompanying

Figure 2. A Released Item from the Delaware State Testing Program (DSTP) with Scoring Tool and Instructional Analysis

---

LIFE SCIENCE

In the Life Science section of the DSTP [Delaware State Testing Program] students are required to figure out the possible gene pairs that come from two parents. Often this type of genetics word problem will require students to explain how dominant and recessive genes affect the way traits are inherited. One of the released items from spring 2000 DSTP illustrates a genetics question students are asked and what is required to earn complete credit.

Analysis:

After analyzing DSTP results from across the State, it appears that many students are struggling with some of the same genetic concepts. For instance, when expected to construct Punnett squares, students fail to separate the gene pair (alleles) of the parents. This error tends to indicate that students are confused as to how meiosis affects the distribution of chromosomes and subsequently genes. Once the students make this kind of mistake it is impossible for them to determine all the gene pairs for a given characteristic that could come from a set of parents. Furthermore, when students end up with gene combinations (inside the squares) that contain more genetic information than the parents it does not seem to cue them into the fact that they have done something wrong in setting up the Punnett square.

Students also experience difficulty with genetic problems when they are given phenotypic patterns of inheritance and asked to derive information about the genotype of an organism (as in the case of the released problem). Again, if students attempt to construct a Punnett square to answer the question they must first be able to determine the genotype for each of the parent organisms and then separate the alleles across the top and down the side of the square. After completing the simple monohybrid crosses they should then be able to apply their understanding of genetics to explain the relationships between the phenotypes and genotypes of the parents and offsprings.

Released Item:

In cats, the gene for short hair (A) is dominant over the gene for long hair (a). A short-haired cat is mated to a long-haired cat, and four kittens are produced, two short-haired and two long-haired. Explain how the two parents could produce these offsprings.

Scoring Tool:

Response must indicate in words and/or in a correctly constructed Punnett square the appropriate genotypes of both parents and the predicted offspring. For example:

2 points: One parent must be heterozygous and therefore, has a 50% chance of giving the short-haired gene and a 50% chance of giving the long-haired gene. The other parent can only give the long-haired gene. Therefore, 50% of the offspring will be long-haired and 50% short-haired. Note: The words "heterozygous" and "homozygous" are not required to receive full credit.

OR

	a	a
A	Aa	Aa
a	aa	aa

(Continues on next page.)

(Figure 2. continued)

OR

Parents: aa x Aa   Offspring: 50% Aa 50% aa

1 point:	Partially correct response, but some flaws may be included. For example, the student may explain the parent with the dominant gene is carrying the recessive allele, but the combinations inside the Punnett square do not reflect separation of the alleles.
0 points:	Incorrect, inappropriate, or incomplete response.

requirements for technical accuracy. When used for high-stakes purposes, tests must be designed with sufficient reliability to yield a stable total score for each student. This means that, within a reasonably small margin of error, students would end up in the same proficiency category if they were retested on the same or closely parallel test.

Reliability does not ensure validity, however. Especially, reliability cannot make up for what's left out of the test or how performance levels might shift if students were allowed to work with familiar hands-on materials, to work in groups, to consult resources, or to engage in any other activities that sharply changed the context of knowledge use. Because no one instrument can be a perfectly valid indicator of student achievement, the professional *Standards for Educational and Psychological Testing* (AERA, APA, NCME 1999) require that high-stakes decisions "not be made on the basis of a single test score" (146). While once-per-year state assessments can be made sufficiently accurate to report to parents about a student's level of achievement, they should not be used solely to determine grade-to-grade promotion or high school graduation.

Can these state proficiency tests also be diagnostic at the level of individual students? The answer is no, at least not in the same way that classroom assessments can be diagnostic. Once-per-year survey tests are perhaps better thought of as "screening" instruments, not unlike the health screenings provided in shopping malls. If one indicator shows a danger signal, the first thing you should do is see your doctor for a more complete and accurate assessment.

The same subtest information that is available for program level profiling may also be useful at the level of individual student profiles. Notice, however, that the instructional insights provided earlier by Wood and Schmidt (2002) were based on state patterns for large numbers of students. For individual students, it would be inappropriate to interpret the results of single items, and even subtest peaks and valleys are often not reliably different. Unfortunately, the most commonly reported profiles do not reveal a particular area of weakness, where a student needs more work. Instead, test results most frequently come back with predictable findings of "low on everything" or "high on everything."

I have explained previously that large-scale tests are too broad to provide (in one or two hours of testing) much detail on a student's knowledge of specific content or skills—such as control of variables, formulating explanations, energy transfer, the effect of heat on chemical reactions, the structure and function of cells, the relationship of diversity and evolution, and so forth. An additional source of difficulty is the match or mismatch between the level of a large-scale test and an individual student's level of functioning. Some state assessment programs are based on basic-skills tests with relatively low-level proficiency standards. Low-level, basic-skills tests provide very little information about the knowledge or knowledge gains of high-performing students. In contrast, in states that built their tests in keeping with the rhetoric of world-class standards, there will be few test items designed to measure the knowledge or knowledge gains of below-grade-level students. NAEP, for example, was designed to measure relatively challenging grade-level content, and therefore yields unreliable total score estimates for students whose performance is below grade level.

I should also emphasize that the item sampling strategies currently used for fillout test frameworks are not designed with an understanding of learning progressions. The authors of *Knowing What Students Know* (Pellegrino, Chudowsky, and Glaser 2001) explained that current curriculum standards "emphasize *what* students should learn, [but] they do not describe *how* students learn in ways that are maximally useful for guiding instruction and assessment" (256). Thus the fourth-grade NAEP mathematics test is a sample of where students are expected to have gotten by fourth grade, not how they got here. Models of student progression in learning have been developed in research settings, but they have not yet been built into large-scale testing programs. It would be a mistake, therefore, to try to make diagnostic decisions from a fine-grained analysis of test results. Especially, one should not assume that students should be instructed on the easy items on the test before proceeding to the difficult items. Such reasoning would tend to reinforce instructional patterns whereby slower students are assigned rote tasks and more able students are assigned reasoning tasks. A more appropriate instructional strategy, based on comprehension research for example, would ask lower-performing students to reason with simpler material rather than delaying reasoning tasks. The appropriate learning continua needed to plan instructional interventions cannot be inferred by rank ordering the item statistics in a traditional test.

Given the inherent limitations of once-per-year, large-scale assessments, there are only a few ways that large-scale assessments could be made more diagnostic for individual students. Out-of-level testing is one possibility. This strategy would still involve a standard test administration, but students would take a test more appropriate to their performance level (such tests are statistically linked across students to provide an accurate total score for a school even though students are taking different tests). The state of Wyoming is one of a few states experimenting with a more ambitious effort to make state assessments more instructionally relevant. Director of Assessment Scott Marion provided the example in Figure 3 of a curriculum-embedded assessment. The state, along with the Wyoming Body of Evidence Activities Consortium, developed 15–18 of these assessments in each of four core areas to be used to determine if students have met the state's graduation standards. Districts are free to use these assessments or to develop their own as long as they meet alignment criteria. The desirable feature of these assessments is that teachers can embed them where they fit best in the high school curriculum, so long as students have had a fair opportunity to learn the necessary material and to demonstrate that learning. "Carmaliticus" could be taken by ninth- or eleventh-grade biology students. Because these tasks exemplify the science standards and are administered in the context of instruction, teachers receive much more immediate and targeted information about student performance than they do from more comprehensive large-scale assessments.

The Wyoming example also illustrates one of the inevitable trade-offs if state assessments were to be made more diagnostic of individual student's learning. More diagnosis means more testing—so as to gather sufficient data in each skill and content area. More testing can perhaps be justified when it is closely tied to specific units of study. But one could not defend the notion of 5–15 hours of testing for a state-level science assessment. A reasonable principle to govern the design of external tests would be the following: either large-scale assessments should be minimally intrusive because they are being administered for program-level data, or large-scale assessments must be able to demonstrate direct benefit to student learning for additional time spent. For policy makers who want more individual pupil diagnosis, this principle leads to the idea of curriculum-embedded assessments administered at variable times so that results can be used in the context of instruction. The only other alternative is for states to develop curriculum materials with sample assessment tasks

---

Figure 3. A Curriculum-Embedded Assessment

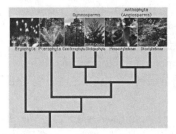

Science Assessment Activity #7:

Carmaliticus

Introduction: To describe evolutionary change and classification systems, scientists use phylogenetic trees. Pictured *[at left]* is an example of the organization of a phylogenetic tree into branches.

Science Assessed:

- Knowledge of classification systems and evolutionary change

- Ability to organize organisms into a phylogenetic tree according to observable characteristics

In this activity, you will take on the role of a scientist developing a phylogenetic tree to represent the evolutionary changes and classification of an imaginary organism called a Carmaliticus.

Attached are the 66 *imaginary* organisms, called Carmaliticus. They are organized according to Eras, indicated in the table below. The organisms and the Eras are *not* related to Earth's geologic time periods or the conditions within earth's time periods.

(Continues on next page.)

Source: Property of the Wyoming Body of Evidence Activities Consortium and the Wyoming Department of Education. Reprinted with permission.

Eras	Organism #	Time in Millions of Years Ago
Era A	66	245–209
Era B	64–65	208–145
Era C	60–64	144–67
Era D	53–59	66–58
Era E	43–52	57–37
Era F	29–42	36–24
Era G	15–28	23–6
Era H	8–14	5–2
Era I	4–7	1–.1
Recent– Still Living	1–3	Present

Part I – Phylogenetic Tree: Organize the Carmalitici into a phylogenetic tree according to Eras and characteristics of the Carmaliticus. On the tree, link each organism to only one organism from the previous Era, with a line; and indicate the extinction of a branch, with a labeled line.

Part II –Written Explanation: Provide a written report with your phylogenetic tree that includes the following:

1) The reasoning you used to make decisions regarding placement of the Carmaliticus and their branches;

2) For *two* branches with *seven or more* Carmaliticus, describe how one organism evolved to another—based on identifiable characteristics of the organisms;

3) Possible environments of *four* Eras, supported with characteristics of the organisms that would justify your decisions;

4) A comparison of your phylogenetic tree to one other tree produced by a classmate. In your comparison, you are to identify at least two significant differences between your tree and the other tree, including a description about the difference in the organization and characteristics of all of the organisms within at least one branch and a comparison of the branches.

NOTE - Important considerations as you develop your phylogenetic tree:

a) Consider the organization of the entire tree before attaching the Carmaliticus.

b) Neatness and spacing will make a difference when you have to examine and explain the individual characteristics and the overall trends of the tree.

c) Based upon assumptions you make in the development of your tree, it is unlikely that you and another classmate will have an identical tree.

d) Each organism should only be tied to one other organism from the previous Era.

(Continues on next page.)

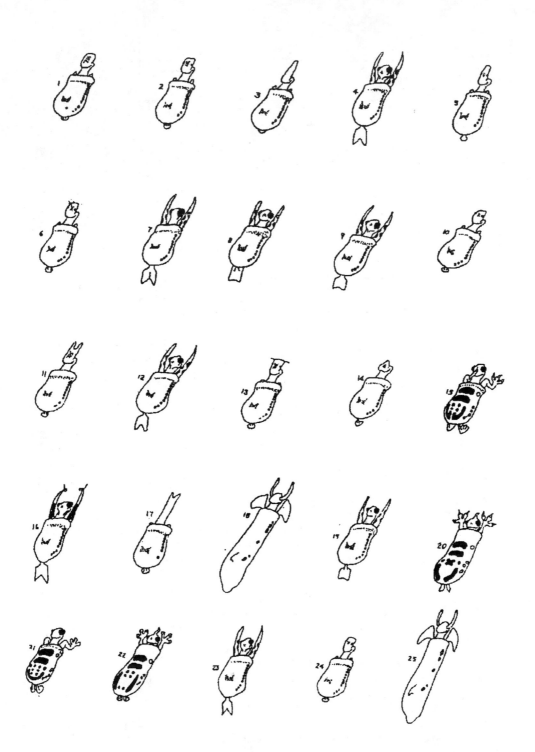

(Continues on next page.)

National Science Teachers Association

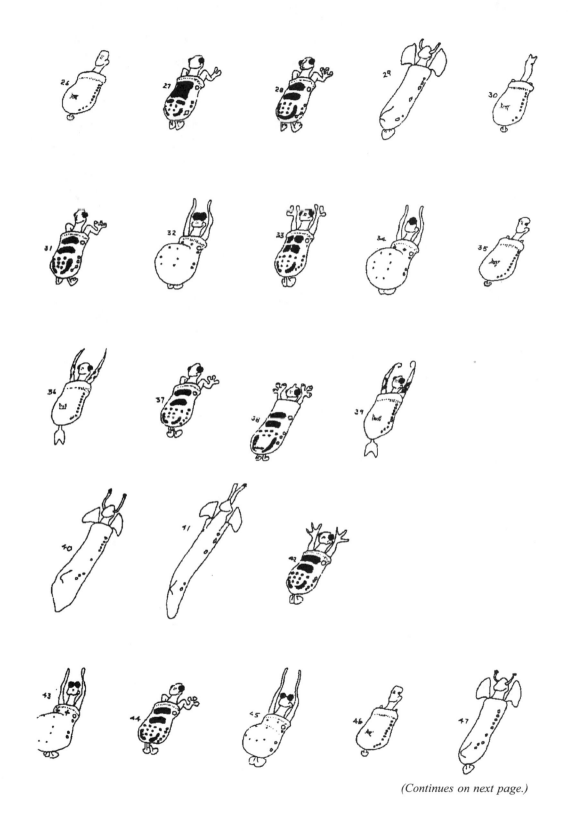

(Continues on next page.)

Everyday Assessment in the Science Classroom

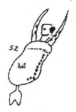

for teachers to use to check on student progress but not to be used in formal data collection.

Professional Development

Professional development associated with standards-based reforms has tended to focus on the intention of the standards (Why should students be able to communicate mathematically?), and on curriculum materials and instructional strategies to implement the standards (What does inquiry-based instruction look like?). Assessment activities tied to standards have the potential to deepen teachers' understandings of the meaning of standards as well as to provide the means to improve student learning. The additional goal of having teachers become more adept at using specific formative assessment strategies can also be furthered by professional development that addresses content standards. There are two important reasons for embedding teachers' learning about assessment in larger professional development efforts—one practical, the other conceptual. First, teachers' time is already overburdened. It is very unlikely that teachers could take time to learn about formative assessment strategies in a way that is not directly tied to the immediate pressures to raise student achievement on accountability tests. Second, assessment efforts only make sense if they are intimately tied to content learning. Therefore, assessment learning can be undertaken in the context of helping teachers improve performance on a state test, so long as we clearly understand the difference between teaching to the standards and teaching the test.

Folklore of advanced placement (AP) examinations has it that some teachers return to Princeton year after year to participate in the scoring of AP exams because of the learning experience. Not only is it important to see what kinds of questions are asked, but it makes one a better teacher to engage with student work and to discuss with one's colleagues how to interpret criteria in light of specific student performances. In this same vein, Wood and Schmidt (2002) describe several different aspects of professional development that occurred in Delaware when teachers were involved in assessment development, pilot testing, and scoring. First and foremost, "teachers became hooked on student learning." By focusing on what students were learning, they moved from being good at delivering inquiry-based instruction to focusing on what students were actually learning from that instruction. For example, teachers learned to use double-digit rubrics that produced both a score and the reason for the score, "which completely transformed our thinking."

> A single-digit rubric just lumps partially correct responses together and doesn't discriminate between the milder and more serious partially correct or wrong responses. The diagnostic rubrics are ordered so that teachers score student work and easily flag the most frequent missteps in student thinking. This kind of diagnostic information is not available from a single-digit rubric that is so holistic that it fails to identify that students get things

wrong or right for different reasons. Making explicit an array of student thinking around a question forces the teachers to think about the implications for instructional practice. This characterization of student learning resonated more with teachers at a gut level than the daunting but somewhat intriguing collection of student thinking documented in the research base. (Wood and Schmidt 2002)

Dr. Maryellen Harmon, a consultant to Wood and Schmidt's (2002) project, required that teachers who were developing summative assessment tasks take time to write out what each item is measuring and also to write out their own "elegant answers" to each question before developing the scoring criteria and rubric. From these "academic exercises," teachers found they could catch flaws in their own thinking and sometimes reconsidered whether the target was even worth measuring in the first place. They also became aware of how students would struggle when they themselves could not agree on what was being asked or required for a complete response. During pilot testing, Dr. Harmon also coached teachers to learn from student responses and not always blame the students when they couldn't respond. Although Wood and Schmidt focused on whether learning from the summative assessment project could be generalized to developing items for the state test, these skills could as likely be generalized to developing better classroom assessment. As a result of these experiences, "teachers were much more willing to pilot potential DSTP [Delaware Student Testing Program] test items prior to submitting them and were more aware of how to interpret student work. Many of these teachers now write out a "what this test measures …" when they construct an item for the state test. They are much less likely to blame a student for an unanticipated response and more likely to reexamine their question and rubric."

The assessment development process and pilot testing experiences described by Wood and Schmidt (2002) show us the power of real professional development opportunities as compared to merely receiving student scores from a state test. "When lead teachers had to score student work from a unit that was just taught, teachers had to evaluate both the extent to which students had acquired certain concepts as well as reflect on their own teaching strategies for particular lessons." For example, "teachers had assumed that students could trace the path of electricity in a complete circuit. When their own data contradicted their assumptions, they realized the need to address this learning in another way with their students." Most tellingly, teachers had to face the dissonance between what they had taught and what students had learned:

After all, these teachers knew that good science was happening in their classrooms—they were using NSF materials, had undergone the training on the modules, and were comfortable with the content knowledge now and employing inquiry-based strategies. The students were active in their learning and enjoyed the lessons immensely. Imagine the impact of data that confronts and challenges their confidence in knowing what their students know. It was Shavelson (also a consultant to the project) who encouraged the leadership to let teachers struggle through this new "problem space" because ultimately that is where all learning occurs. An opportunity to discuss not only their students' learning but similarly situated students' learning with other teachers using the same units has proven to be a key ingredient for realizing Fullan's idea of assessment conversations and is a more powerful mode of professional development than learning the modules and inquiry-based teaching without this aspect. (Wood and Schmidt 2002)

To summarize, then, professional development focused on assessment of student learning can be a powerful tool to help teachers move beyond merely implementing inquiry activities to an increased awareness of what their students are getting from the activities. Given the layers of assessment-related demands already faced by teachers, efforts to improve classroom assessment strategies should be woven into standards-based professional development and curriculum development. Teachers need better access to materials that model teaching for understanding—with extended instructional activities, formative assessment tasks, scoring rubrics, and summative assessments built in. And, as illustrated by Wood and Schmidt's (2002) experiences, they need extended support while attempting to use these materials and draw inferences about how to improve instruction.

Conclusion: Impediments and Recommendations

The single most important requirement to increase the likelihood that large-scale assessments will contribute positively to student learning is to improve the substance of what is assessed. If large-scale assessments were to embody important learning goals—not only inquiry skills, but also the important big ideas in content areas, geological time scale, photosynthesis, why electric current is different from "flowing" water, why we isolate smallpox patients and not AIDS patients—then other aspects of the assessment, such as program evaluation profiles, released item insights, and professional development, can also be used to improve instruction. In *Knowing What Students Know*, Pellegrino, Chudowsky, and Glaser (2001) argued that for an assessment system to support learning, it has to have the feature of *coherence*. That means that classroom and external assessments have to share the same or compatible underlying models of student learning; otherwise, as in the present-day system, they will work at cross purposes.

While a large-scale assessment might be based on a model of learning that is coarser than that underlying the assessments used in classrooms, the conceptual base for the large-scale assessment should be a broader version of one that makes sense at the finer-grained level (Mislevy 1996). In this way, the external assessment results will be consistent with the more detailed understanding of learning underlying classroom instruction and assessment. (Pellegrino, Chudowsky, and Glaser 2001, 255–56)

In attempting to pursue this vision of an ideal assessment system, science educators should be aware of several potential obstacles:

- Cost

- The No Child Left Behind Act's mandate for testing every pupil (with no out-of-level testing)

- Technical standards and legal protections

- Curriculum control

- Lack of trust of teachers as evaluators

- Beliefs held by policy makers about standards-based reform

- Mechanical data systems

Substantively ambitious assessments can be developed and scored reliably for large-scale purposes, but they invariably cost more than machine-scored, multiple-choice tests. Passage of the No Child Left Behind Act has so markedly increased the amount of testing required that we are likely to see a continuing decline in the substantive quality of large-scale tests, because state agencies often cannot afford to do better. Science educators have the advantage that science will be assessed less frequently than reading and mathematics, and therefore, it is more feasible to advocate for high-quality science assessments. Technical standards and legal protections also tend to work against the quality of assessments simply because trivial things are more easily measured consistently. Therefore, the case will have to be made as to why better assessments are worth the investment (i.e., why it's worth it to spend the extra money to measure important things consistently).

Other obstacles to assessment reform include issues of curriculum control and lack of trust of teachers as evaluators. Successful implementations of substantively ambitious assessments, such as the New Standards Project (1997) and the Educational Testing Service's Pacesetter program, have moved much closer to curriculum development than traditional test construction, which merely collected test items. A problem arises then, when states make the tests and districts control curriculum, about how to achieve the kind of coherence envisioned by Pellegrino, Chudowsky, and Glaser (2001). Similarly, teachers gain more from assessments when they are involved in providing data, and teacher participation makes it more likely that assessments can include extended tasks grounded in classroom work. Therefore, including portfolio and project data would increase the validity and meaningfulness of a large-scale assessment. But because of distrust, which motivates the accountability movement in the first place, proponents of substantively richer assessments will have to think of safeguards, such as score moderation schemes that verify the accuracy of teacher-reported data, to counter the claim that teachers might misrepresent student achievement.

Finally, there is the difficulty that policy makers may hold very different beliefs about standards-based reform than those who originally advocated for conceptually linked curriculum and assessment reforms. While originators like Smith and O'Day (1990) and Resnick and Resnick (1992) were clear about the need for what they called *capacity building*, including substantial professional development for teachers, many present-day policy makers have adopted an economic incentives model as their underlying theory of the reform. Those holding the latter view are unlikely to see the need to invest in curriculum development or professional training. Add to this picture the fact that "data-driven instruction" is being marketed more aggressively than are rich assessment and curriculum units. Using data to guide instruction is, of course, a good thing. Investing in mechanical data systems is a mistake, however, if they are built on bad tests. There is no point in getting detailed disaggregations of test data when test content bears little resemblance to valued curriculum. Trying to make sense of this cacophonous scene will be difficult. What one should advocate for will clearly be different in each state depending on the quality of the existing large-scale assessment and likelihood of persuading state-level decision makers to invest in instructionally relevant curriculum development and professional training.

If science educators want to move toward large-scale assessment that is conceptually linked to classroom learning, what should they be *for?* They should advocate for a good test that embodies the skills and conceptual understandings called for in the science standards. A rich and challenging assessment could take the form of curriculum-embedded assessments or be a combination of state-level, on-demand assessments and local embedded assessments, projects, and portfolios as in the New Standards Project (1997). As advocated in *Knowing What Students Know* (Pellegrino, Chudowsky, and Glaser 2001), there should be a strong substantive coherence between what is called for in the state assessment and what is elaborated in local instructional units and classroom assessments. To realize the full potential for teacher learning, professional development should be provided that uses the power of assessment to look at student work and to redesign instruction accordingly. Teachers should have access to curriculum materials that reflect inquiry-based instruction with well-conceived assessment tools built in. And they should have supported opportunities to try out new instructional materials and formative assessment strategies.

What if the state has a bad test? Then the strategies for science educators should be quite different. In fact, the goal should be to reinvigorate the intended goals for learning and to be explicit about what would be left out if we focused narrowly on the curriculum implied by the test. Groups of teachers or curriculum specialists might want to go through this exercise of mapping the state test to the science standards. Then they could ask, What support is needed to ensure that instruction focuses on the standards rather than the test, and what evidence will we provide to parents and school board members to educate them about important accomplishments not reflected in the test?

Ultimately the goal of any assessment should be to further student learning. Classroom assessments have the greatest potential for directly improving learning because they can be located in the midst of instruction and can provide timely feedback at just the point of a student's uncertainty or incomplete mastery. Large-scale assessments can also support the learning process, but to do this they must faithfully elicit the knowledge, skills, and reasoning abilities that we hope for students to develop, and they must be linked in a well-articulated way to ongoing program evaluation and professional development.

References

American Educational Research Association (AERA), American Psychological Association (APA), National Council on Measurement in Education (NCME). 1999. *Standards for educational and psychological testing.* Washington, DC: American Educational Research Association.

Atkin, J. M., P. Black, and J. Coffey. 2001. *Classroom assessment and the national science education standards.* Washington, DC: National Academy Press.

Black, P., and D. Wiliam.1998. Assessment and classroom learning. *Assessment in Education* 5(1): 7–74.

California Department of Education. 1994. *A sampler of science assessment.* Sacramento: California Department of Education.

Fredericksen, J. R., and A. Collins. 1989. A systems approach to educational testing. *Educational Researcher* 18: 27–32.

Mislevy, R. J. 1996. Test theory reconceived. *Journal of Educational Measurement* 33(4): 379–416.

National Research Council (NRC). 1996. *National science education standards.* Washington, DC: National Academy Press.

New Standards Project. 1997. *Performance standards: English language arts, mathematics, science, applied learning.* Vols. 1–3. Washington, DC: National Center for Education Statistics and the University of Pittsburgh.

Pellegrino, J. W., N. Chudowsky, and R. Glaser. 2001. *Knowing what students know: The science and design of educational assessment.* Washington, DC: National Academy Press.

Resnick, L. B., and D. P. Resnick. 1992. Assessing the thinking curriculum: New tools for educational reform. In *Changing assessments: Alternative views of aptitude, achievement, and instruction.* Boston: Kluwer.

Sadler, R. 1989. Formative assessment and the design of instructional systems. *Instructional Science* 18: 119–44.

Shepard, L. A. 2000. The role of assessment in a learning culture. *Educational Researcher* 29(7): 4–14.

Smith, M. S., and J. O'Day. 1990. Systemic school reform. In *Politics of education association yearbook 1990,* 233–67. London: Taylor and Francis.

Stipek, D. J. 1996. Motivation and instruction. In *Handbook of educational psychology,* eds. D. C. Berliner and R. C. Calfee, 85–113. New York: Macmillan.

Whaley, M. 2002. Owens looks to broaden CSAP focus: Governor wants student-performance test to become tool for individual improvement. *Denver Post,* 14 March.

Wood, R., and J. Schmidt. 2002. History of the development of Delaware Comprehensive Assessment Program in Science. Unpublished memorandum.

Reflections on Assessment

F. James Rutherford

James Rutherford recently retired from the American Association for the Advancement of Science, where he was chief education officer and the originator and director of Project 2061. Leading up to that position, he was a teacher of high school science, president of the National Science Teachers Association, professor of science education at Harvard University and at New York University, assistant director of the National Science Foundation, and assistant secretary of the U.S. Department of Education. He also initiated and directed the Carnegie Science-Humanities Project, Harvard Project Physics, and Project City Science.

Perhaps it is the battle cry for "accountability." Or perhaps it is the infusion of the empirical spirit of science into all walks of life. Maybe it is simply the natural offspring of "standards." But whatever the cause, *assessment* has become the educational issue of the day. Hence this National Science Teachers Association compilation of essays by leaders in the field of educational assessment.

This particular chapter consists of comments and questions triggered by my reading of Chapters 1 through 9. The first two sections below expand briefly on notions that I believe provide a larger context for "everyday classroom assessment." One notion is that there is now considerable confusion on the assessment scene due to mounting demands, conflicting expectations, daunting constraints, and lack of agreement on the need for and character of K–12 assessment in science. The other claim I wish to make is that there simply is no one best method of assessment and that each must be considered critically in terms of the main purpose it is intended to serve. I conclude by suggesting some questions for readers to consider as they discuss with one another the claims and propositions set out in this book.

The Changing Assessment Scene

Assessment—"testing" in simpler times—is not, of course, something new on the educational scene. Quite the opposite, for it has surely been around in one form or another for as long as teaching itself. But since the Second World War the circumstances bearing on educational assessment have changed dramatically. These circumstances have included rapid demographic shifts, increasing educational demands, the accumulation of findings from cognitive research, and the episodic nature of post-war efforts to improve science education in response to a sequence of national crises attributed to the failure of American schools.

Demographics

It is difficult enough to determine how each child is progressing in classrooms in which the students share similar social, economic, language, and cultural backgrounds. And it is often equally difficult to know what action to take in response to assessment outcomes. Imagine, then, how vastly more difficult assessment (and basing teaching on assessment results) must be when, as in today's schools, the students differ greatly from one another in so many ways.

From time to time, the medical metaphor—often disguised linguistically—re-surfaces in education circles, for surely in principle it makes sense. (Feasibility, however, is another matter.) Teachers are essentially advised to "diagnose" each student's learning condition and then to "prescribe" individual remedies to respond to the diagnosis. Not surprisingly, in time the idea fades away for a while, since teachers are not yet really in a position to either diagnose or treat with precision. Assessment can detect whether or not a student has learned something, but rarely determine the depth and sophistication of the learning, and certainly not whether the learning is temporary or lasting. In any case, an assessment showing defective learning is not a diagnosis, anymore than the detection of high blood pressure is. And treatment depends on a body of dependable clinical research findings and codified experience that, in education, have yet to reach the level of that found in medical practice.

This is not to counsel despair but rather to urge caution in setting assessment goals. With greater investment in the development of assessment procedures and research on learning, substantial advancement can be made over the next few decades, gradually providing teachers with an increasingly scientific basis for their work. In the meantime, it is well to remember that while it has put new—and not yet well understood—demands on teaching and assessment, the extreme student diversity now in our schools is valuable precisely because it is a reflection of the demographics of our society. Any assessment approach that does not make thoughtful efforts to take the changing demographics explicitly into account should be viewed with skepticism.

Educational Demands

By the end of the Second World War, the United States was well on the way to shifting from an economy based largely on agriculture to one based increasingly on industrial manufacturing and commerce. The schools in time responded to that change. "Shop" became "industrial arts," for instance, and the proportion of students taking the college preparatory curriculum and graduating from high school increased. The status of science education grew, and as it did, more students took science than before, and new content was added to the existing science and mathematics courses.

This trend—think of it as expecting more science and mathematics from more students—was accelerated with the shift to the so-called information-based economy and rapid advances in science. Still more new content, therefore, was added to existing science courses (little content ever being removed, subtraction seemingly out of the question in education), and advanced placement courses proliferated. Thus even in the face of a K–12 student body that was becoming progressively more diverse—with a greater percentage of students with learning disabilities and of students (particularly in rural and inner-city schools) from low socioeconomic families and immigrant families from Third World countries—the curriculum became more demanding.

As we well know, ambitious national education standards were eventually formulated to codify these rising expectations, followed by state standards that are more or less based on the national standards, followed by legislation requiring more testing more often of more students. It is interesting to note, by way of contrast, that in California just prior to the war (at which time, incidentally, California was widely regarded, whether correctly or not, as having the country's leading educational system), students faced no examinations other than those that individual teachers themselves decided to give. It would seem that as confidence in schools and teachers shrinks, the demand for testing grows—or could it be the other way around?

Learning Studies

The working assumption of teachers through the decades has been that they could determine accurately how well their students were learning what they were being taught. That is what all those final examinations are about. But beginning in the late 1970s researchers started looking more closely at learning, and in due course the research findings started showing up in refereed journals. After such studies had accumulated for about a decade, Project 2061, the long-range reform project of the American Association for the Advancement of Science (AAAS), examined all of the cognitive science research literature (in English, and some in other languages) dealing with science, mathematics, and technology learning at the K–12 ages (AAAS 1993).

The picture that emerged was not reassuring. For one thing, it turned out that the studies were not well distributed but strongly skewed toward physics and mathematics. Furthermore, the published papers were uneven: some met rigorous scientific standards but many—as determined by an external panel of researchers—were flawed methodologically, and therefore not sound enough to be used in the AAAS analysis. What the review told us is that we had a long way to go before we had as much trustworthy knowledge as we would like, in a scientific sense, about what students *actually* learn as a consequence of K–12 science instruction. This has been generally borne out since then in the cognitive literature on science and mathematics learning (AAAS 1997).

More disturbing, perhaps, the research seems to show that students take away from school most of the mistaken science notions with which they started. In short, they seem not to learn what we think we have taught them. Unfortunately, relatively few teachers are well enough informed on the common misconceptions students harbor to take them seriously into account in their teaching. This is dramatically borne out in a series of videos produced by the Harvard-Smithsonian Center for Astrophysics. For example, the first of these, *A Private Universe*, demonstrates that upon graduation even Harvard students, most of whom had attended the nation's most prestigious private and public schools, still hold inaccurate ideas about what causes the seasons and the phases of the moon. Not to be outdone by their crosstown rivals, new MIT graduates were found to give wrong answers to the question of where the mass of a log comes from. (These videos are available from the Annenberg/CPB Math and Science Collection, P.O. Box 2345, S. Burlington, VT 05407-7373.)

At the very least, learning studies reveal that we must be very careful indeed in making claims about what students have learned. They also demonstrate just how difficult it is to determine learning outcomes convincingly. This, in turn, suggests that we need to develop an array of assessment approaches that may not be as scientifically rigorous as those used in cognitive science but that are explicitly designed to serve different assessment purposes. And in the bargain, we need to develop ways of assessing *them*—which is to say ways of *assessing the assessments*—rather than uncritically accepting their validity and reliability. In sum, serious learning studies have complicated the assessment picture but have clarified both the limits and promise of assessment.

National Crises

There is always reason enough to evaluate carefully what learning is taking place in our schools and to report the results honestly to those who have a legitimate interest in knowing. Ideally, educators should be expected to work continuously, year after year, at improving the teaching, curriculum, and teaching materials in the nation's schools. To accomplish that, they need to work steadily to improve their ability to assess student progress accurately. But steady, continuous upgrading of assessment has not been the reality—not, at least, in the United States.

As it turns out, most reform efforts in science education—including those focusing on assessment—seem to be driven by a sense of national crises. Hence serious attention to testing is episodic rather than continuous and carried out in an atmosphere of urgency and distrust. There has never been a time when American K–12 education was not sharply criticized, the subject usually being the "basics" of reading, writing, and arithmetic or the feud between the advocates of "life adjustment" and "liberal arts" curricula. For some classics in this genre, see *Educational Wastelands* (Bestor 1953), *Quackery in the Public Schools* (Lynd 1953), and *Education and Freedom* (Rickover 1959). However, in times of national crises, real or imagined, for which education takes the blame, deserved or not, the charges of inadequacy become more shrill and ubiquitous.

With the end of the Second World War, the importance of science and mathematics (as distinct from basic arithmetic) education came into sharp focus. In 1950, the National Science Foundation came into being, charged by Congress with supporting the advancement of science *education* as well as scientific research. The nation was, it seemed at the time, on its way to the radical improvement of science and mathematics education.

But in fact the public was not yet quite ready for science education reform on a national scale. Some reform projects got underway in the late 1950s, notably the Physical Science Study Committee in 1956 and the Biological Sciences Curriculum Committee in 1958 (Randolph 2002). Most of the dozens of "alphabet" reform projects (and the summer and academic year institutes for science and math teachers associated with them) followed a bit later, owing their existence to the shock of *Sputnik* in October 1959. That disturbing Soviet Cold War accomplishment quickly became the basis of a national *educational* crisis no less than an engineering one. We were falling behind the Soviet Union, the press and public opinion soon had it, because our schools were inferior and had let us down by not producing more scientists and engineers. The response was an unprecedented national effort to boost American science and mathematics education at every level. The nation was now truly on its way to science education reform.

Crises, however, have a tendency to go away. Reaching the Moon first had become accepted in the United States as the definitive test of which country would win the space race. The United States won that race decisively, and, with the sense of crises gone, the science education reform movement coasted to a halt. There were, to be sure, other factors leading to the decline of interest in the reform movement. Among them, for example, was the rancorous debate over "Man, A Course of Study," a social studies reform project of the period. *The Transformation of the School: Progressivism in American Education, 1876-1957* (Cremin 1961) provides a historical perspective preceding the *Sputnik* episode. Subsequent developments can be found in *Schoolhouse Politics: Lessons from the Sputnik Era* (Dow 1991) and *The Troubled Crusade: American Education, 1945–1980* (Ravitch 1983).

But the main point here is that many of the initiatives of the *Sputnik*-era reform projects—among them the efforts of the projects to come up with more meaningful approaches to assessment—did not have time to mature and become entrenched in the schools before political support for them largely disappeared.

Instances of novel approaches to assessment can be found in the materials of many of the projects and are best examined in conjunction with the instructional components of each, especially since some concentrated on assessing performance rather than acquired knowledge. Two examples can be drawn from the Project Physics Course developed at Harvard University. In one case, instructors showed students the same filmed, real-life events at the beginning and end of the course and asked them to describe in writing what they saw and to offer explanations for what happened in the film. Conceptual and language changes were to provide evidence of what physics principles had been learned. This technique showed promise, but the demise of the reform movement made it impossible at the time to obtain support to pursue this line of research further. (Needless to say, the development of computer technology has now made it possible to develop powerful interactive assessment activities that go far beyond the limited possibilities of 16mm film.)

The Project Physics Course also developed a set of *student-choice* examinations. Each of the six units making up the course was accompanied by a booklet containing four different tests from which students could individually select the one they felt would best allow them to display what they had learned. The four tests differed from each other in style and emphasis: One was entirely multiple choice, one was made up of problems and essay questions, and two were a combination of objective and subjective styles, with one emphasizing the historical, philosophical, and social aspects of the content and the other the quantitative and experimental. The idea was to move teachers away from comparing students and toward assessing individual students in terms of their progress based on their own expression of what they had learned.

After a reform lull, another crisis provoked another energetic round of K–12 science education reform. The economies of Japan and Germany seemed to be surpassing the U.S. economy. This, too, was attributed largely to the failure of the American public schools. The spirit of the time was fully captured in the influential report *A Nation at Risk* (U.S. Department of Education 1983). But the U.S. economy eventually reasserted itself (for which, by the way, education received no credit), and once again the reform movement slackened. Eventually, a new and quite different crisis came to the rescue: An international study documented how badly we do in school science and mathematics compared to other nations (Schmidt, McKnight, and Raizen 1997). Reform was on again—this time an educational crisis provoked by educational assessment itself. It is still in play, and hence too early to tell how long it will last and what form it will settle on. It is clear, however, that this on-again-off-again commitment to K–12 education reform has made it difficult to sustain a serious effort long enough to accomplish lasting reforms in general, let alone in science education assessment practices.

A result of all of this—demographic changes, increasing learning demands, the revelations of cognitive research, and the spasm-like ups and downs of reform—is assessment in disarray, if not quite chaos. Presidents and governors, federal and state legislatures, CEOs of great business enterprises, newspaper editors, and syndicated columnists are again vocal in demanding school reform.

But the voices are not nearly in harmony. Many assert that the only way we can regain confidence in the schools is for them to provide the nation with hard evidence that our students surpass those in other countries, becoming, as it was famously put by the U.S. governors in 1989, the best in the world by the year 2000 (U.S. Department of Education 1989). Others take the position that the only way to motivate the education system to do better is to confront the schools with frequent and demanding external tests. Then there are those (not too numerous at the moment) who argue for less external testing on the grounds that the real problem is the quality of assessment policies and procedures. And in the background, educators themselves are not of a mind on such science assessment issues as (a) testing for content knowledge versus testing for inquiry skills and (b) assessment against fixed standards versus against "the curve."

Assessment Purposes

The turmoil in the current assessment scene is exacerbated, I believe, by the failure of many of those who are demanding assessment-based accountability to recognize that every form of assessment has its own capabilities, limitations, and side effects and that no single approach is best for all educational purposes (see Paul Black, Chapter 1 in this book). To be effective, assessment should be designed with a clear view of just what service it is intended to perform and for whom. Assessment that is appropriate for helping teachers improve classroom teaching and learning (the subject of this book) is significantly different from assessment that is appropriate for informing parents and certain others persons of student performance or for determining how well the nation's schools or those in a given state or local system are doing (AAAS 2001c).

Improving Classroom Teaching and Learning

The overriding purpose of classroom teaching is to promote student learning of selected understandings and skills. To that end, teachers need to determine how each student is progressing, as well as how the class as a whole is doing, and then know what to do with that information in order to improve teaching and learning. That is a daunting task, but clearly the more direct and immediate the feedback that teachers are able to obtain on student progress, the better situated they are to adjust their teaching, if necessary, to get better results. In this sense, assessing student learning is also assessing teacher performance.

But no less than external testing, classroom assessment can be intrusive and have unwanted side effects, such as distracting students and wasting time. Its use as punishment is, alas, not unknown. It can persuade students that the teacher's role is more to assess them than to help them learn. At risk is the trust that should exist between teachers and their students, a trust that is akin to that between physicians and their patients and between lawyers and their clients. Because thoughtful and purposive assessment is so important for improving classroom teaching and learning, and yet so prone to misuse, the professional training of teachers should arm them with a sophisticated view of assessment and with the knowledge and assessment skills they will need to be effective teachers.

The previous chapters in this book describe aspects of an approach to classroom assessment that is minimally intrusive and closely connected to the content and skills being taught; the approach also contributes to the ability of students and teachers to evaluate their own performance and act on that knowledge. It should be kept in mind, however, that classroom assessment of the sort discussed in those chapters can, at best, produce weak estimates of the performance of any larger dimension of the educational system, such as the school, school district, state, or nation. But of course, by the same token, externally formulated, high-stakes tests can contribute little to individual student learning in the science classroom.

Informing Parents and Others

Most of the time, a very special and sensitive relationship exists between teachers and their students, which is why classroom assessment must be handled with such care. But that relationship does not exist in total isolation. Certain other persons outside the classroom have a need (and a right) to know about individual student performance. Foremost among these, of course, are parents. In addition, at some point university admission officers or prospective employers will want the kind of information about applicants that can be used in making admission and employment decisions.

Note that for these purposes, detailed information of the sort appropriate for improving teaching and learning is rarely needed. Parents are generally satisfied with letter grades and discussions with teachers regarding the progress (and behavior) of their children. As for admission officers and employers, such information as courses taken, grades, honors, activities, teacher recommendations, attendance patterns, and SAT scores are sufficient. Thus third parties have little need for the intimate details of learning that are so necessary for teachers and students.

On the other hand, one might expect that parents would care greatly about how their children do on statewide or national tests relative to other children, and indeed that seems to be the case. Unfortunately, such tests reveal less about individual student learning than what well-prepared teachers can provide on the basis of their own assessments over the year. It may be that teachers and school administrators will have to become better able to help parents put student performance on external tests in a broad assessment perspective. Moreover, external tests should not be allowed by educators or parents to displace careful ongoing assessment by classroom teachers.

Determining System Performance

Just as parents have a right to have informed appraisals of the educational progress of their children, so, too, does society have a right to have informed appraisals of how well its schools are performing. For that purpose, national, state, and school district assessments are appropriate. They must, however, be carefully designed. That includes covering the explicitly defined learning goals set out by the appropriate authorities and using valid statistical and sampling techniques. Since the basic purpose of external testing is to find out how schools in some *aggregate* (national, state, or district) are doing, and not individual students, there is simply no need to conduct such assessments in every subject every year, or to test all students, or to have all of the students who do participate respond to the same set of test items. This seems not to be well understood by the general public.

Indeed, in addition to the huge and quite unnecessary costs, testing all students has a severe functional drawback. Testing all students actually reveals *less* about institutional performance than testing only some students. Blanket testing can sample only a small fraction of the subject matter in question and as a practical matter must be multiple choice and machine scored. By contrast, basing state and national assessments on a stratified random sample of test takers means that the entire sweep of the targeted matter can be covered, since each student faces only a small portion of the test items. And it makes it possible to include some performance testing (which is prohibitively expensive and difficult to score if taken by all students).

Assessing Curriculum Materials

If classroom or external assessment shows that students are not meeting our learning expectations, ineffective classroom practices may not be the reason, or at least not the only reason. The failure may well be due to inadequate curricula. At any one time, many individuals and institutions (though more at some times than at others, depending on the national sense of urgency and the level of support from federal agencies and private foundations) are developing new courses and materials (the stuff of curricula). Claims made for improved learning resulting from the use of the products of these efforts should not, however, be taken at face value. They should, rather, be critically evaluated for their instructional effectiveness.

Since the 1960s most nationally funded curriculum development projects in science education have carried out some assessment in the very process of developing their materials. Feedback from limited field trials enables developers to improve their products before they are released for general use. Carefully conducted formative assessment contributes to the credibility of the claims made for new products and techniques, as well as, usually, to the creation of better products (AAAS 2001a). Still, such assessment is not entirely sufficient for making informed decisions on the adoption of those materials. Arms-length assessment in the context of actual use is also desirable, though difficult to carry out for both technical and practical reasons.

Curriculum assessment is related to but different from assessment for improving classroom teaching and learning, informing third parties, and judging system effectiveness. The constraints are formidable. Any attempt to evaluate curriculum courses and materials must be narrowly focused, and yet cannot escape being affected by the many other variables at play in real-world schools. And of course getting unbiased test schools and controls is difficult and expensive.

Because of such constraints, few curriculum projects have been able to conduct rigorous field studies. Indeed, the Project Physics Course developed at Harvard University may be the only reform project of the *Sputnik* era (or later) whose summative assessment included selecting participating schools using a stratified random sample of all high schools in the United States, assigning schools to test and control groups randomly, and providing similar incentives to the teachers and schools in both the test and control groups.

The summative evaluation of the Project Physics Course used all of its associated print and multimedia materials, but the course textbook was the center of attention (Holton, Rutherford, and Watson 1970). In ordinary circumstances, however, textbooks and their associated teacher and student handbooks stand in as proxies for a course and its supplementary materials. Fortunately, there are degrees of materials assessment that, while short of a completely rigorous assessment based on student use, can provide valuable assurance that the claims made for it are reasonable (AAAS 2001b; Kesidou and Roseman 2002).

Regardless of the scale and rigor of the assessment of curricula, what must be clear from the outset are the intended relationships among learning goals, the curriculum, and assessment (AAAS 2001d). It is a question of priority. Is the intent to have assessment align with the curriculum (a popular choice), which has been independently designed to serve specified learning goals? Or is assessment intended to align with learning goals and drive the curriculum? Or should curriculum and assessment both derive from goals, rather than from each other? The choice makes a difference especially in shaping the form and purpose of classroom assessment.

Considering *Everyday Assessment in the Science Classroom*

As a way of fostering productive discussion of this book, this chapter ends with questions rather than conclusions. Readers of the book will surely have general questions such as these: Are the assessment claims in the chapters clearly identified and explicitly stated? Do the claims made in the separate chapters fit together to present a coherent view of classroom assessment? Are the *validity, feasibility,* and *policy consequences* of the book's propositions satisfactorily addressed?

More particularly:

- *Is it clear what is being proposed with regard to classroom assessment?* Is science classroom assessment presented as just a particular context for classroom assessment or as something rather unique in principle? Is the terminology used sufficiently precise for conveying unambiguously the meaning of the various propositions? Is the relationship between the assessment approach being advocated and the science learning goals made clear?

- *How persuasive are the claims made in this book?* To what extent are the arguments made in support of the various claims anecdotal? To what extent is the evidence presented quantitative? In each case, was the criterion for success specifically stated ahead of time, only implied, or left unspecified? If stated, was it the acquisition by students of specific science knowledge and skills, the acquisition of general learning skills, interpersonal and social skills, or something else? Are procedures described in enough detail to enable independent replications? Are these themselves replications of earlier studies? If so, do the findings support the earlier studies or throw them into doubt? How implicated in the classroom events were the authors themselves, and how does that affect the credibility of the findings?

- *How practical are the proposals in this book?* Would the approaches described in this book work with teachers who were not volunteers? Would they work without the help of university faculty? Without special financial resources beyond the standard school operating budget? Does the application of the approaches to assessment advocated here require extensive retraining of the current population of K–12 teachers? If it is desirable for preservice teacher education to inculcate these practices, will it require university schools of education to change their programs significantly? What incentives would it take for them to do so?

- *What policy issues are implicit in the approach to classroom assessment set forth in this book?* If different teachers of the same science course use the approach described here, can the results be used to compare the aggregate performance of their respective students? If not, how can school administrators and school boards decide on its acceptability? Is this approach to science classroom assessment likely to be at odds with state-mandated assessment? And, finally, do the results of such classroom assessment provide evidence of how well students, individually and collectively, are meeting national science content standards?

References

American Association for the Advancement of Science (AAAS). 1993. *Benchmarks for science literacy*, 327–77. New York: Oxford University Press.

———. 1997. *Resources for science literacy*, 43–58. New York: Oxford University Press.

———. 2001a. *Designs for science literacy*, 129–41. New York: Oxford University Press.

———. 2001b. *Designs for science literacy*, 195.

———. 2001c. *Designs for science literacy*, 201–202.

———. 2001d. *Designs for science literacy*, 203–208.

Bestor, A. E. 1953. *Educational wastelands*. Urbana: University of Illinois Press.

Cremin, L. A. 1961. *The transformation of the school: Progressivism in American education, 1876–1957*. New York: Alfred A. Knopf.

Dow, P. B. 1991. *Schoolhouse politics: Lessons from the Sputnik era*. Cambridge: Harvard University Press.

Holton, G., F. J. Rutherford, and F. G. Watson. 1970. *Project physics*. New York: Holt, Rinehart, and Winston.

Kesidou, S., and J. Roseman. 2002. How well do middle school science programs measure up? Findings from Project 2061's curriculum review study. *Journal of Research in Science Teaching* 39 (6): 522–49.

Lynd, A. 1953. *Quackery in the public schools*. Boston: Little, Brown.

Randolph, J. L. 2002. *Scientists in the classroom: The Cold War reconstruction of American science education*. New York: Palgrave.

Ravitch, D. 1983. *The troubled crusade: American education, 1945–1980*. New York: Basic Books.

Rickover, H. G. 1959. *Education and freedom*. New York: Dutton.

Schmidt, W. H., C. C. McKnight, and S. A. Raizen. 1997. *A splintered vision: An investigation of U.S. science and mathematics education*. Boston: Kluwer.

U.S. Department of Education. 1983. *A nation at risk*. Washington, DC: U.S. Government Printing Office.

———. 1989. *The president's education summit with governors: Joint statement*. Washington, DC: U.S. Government Printing Office.

Index

Page numbers in **boldface** type indicate tables or figures.

National Science Teachers Association